# England in the Middle Ages

*A Captivating Guide to English History During the Medieval Period and Magna Carta*

# Contents

# Free Bonus from Captivating History (Available for a Limited time)

Hi History Lovers!

Now you have a chance to join our exclusive history list so you can get your first history ebook for free as well as discounts and a potential to get more history books for free! Simply visit the link below to join.

Captivatinghistory.com/ebook

Also, make sure to follow us on Facebook, Twitter and Youtube by searching for Captivating History.

# Part 1: Medieval England

*A Captivating Guide to English History in the Middle Ages, Including Events Such as the Norman Conquest, Black Death, and Hundred Years' War*

# Introduction

Medieval England's history starts with the fall of the Roman Empire in the 5th century. However, it is required to briefly get acquainted with the history of the English territories under the Romans, as they had tremendous influence over the development of English society, religion, and state. What followed the fall of the Roman Empire was a collapse of the economy that led to the abandonment of many towns and villages. After the Romans, Germanic tribes turned their attention towards England, where they saw not only opportunity to plunder, but also fertile lands to inhabit. The new identity of England emerged from Germanic immigration. Cultures began to mix, thus developing into a unique identity for the kingdoms of England. Art flourished under the Anglo-Saxon rule, poems such as *Beowulf* were written, and metalwork transformed from a simple craft to a sophisticated art. Even though Christianity had been present in England since Roman times, the Anglo-Saxons were converted only around the 7th century, building numerous monasteries and churches. These monasteries held riches in silver and gold relics, which attracted Vikings who regularly raided them. The fighting with the Danes lasted for several decades. It resulted in the emergence of Wessex as the most powerful Anglo-Saxon kingdom and the creation of a united English identity. Despite the power transfer from Anglo-Saxons to Danes, England emerged as a very powerful, militarily and economically prosperous European kingdom of the 11th century.

In the 11th century, the Anglo-Saxon elite was completely replaced by the invading Normans. William the Conqueror and his successors brought novelties to England such as castles and cavalry. They retained the old English administration, as it was more developed than the one of Normandy. French language and nobility were common at the English royal court, and the kings had their ancestry in France. Usually, they grew up and were educated in France, some of them setting foot on English soil for the first time only after being proclaimed king. England's population more than doubled during the 12th and 13th centuries. The cities started growing and villages expanding, trade was booming, and the economy was stable. However, not everything was right in the kingdom. Kings often clashed with the church in a struggle for power, which led to a series of ecclesiastical reforms. The English government and law developed expeditiously under Anglo-Norman rule, but constant fighting between the barons of England led to uprisings, civil wars, and the loss of Normandy.

The last phase of Medieval England started with the great Famine and Black Death in the 14th century, when millions of lives were lost, resulting in England losing half of its population. The economy was in chaos, and the old political order was crumbling. More uprisings and revolts ensued as the people expressed their dissatisfaction. Life for a commoner shifted from villages to cities, where new opportunities waited. New technologies were introduced, which allowed people to gather knowledge and skill. In this period, many philosophers and healers were sprouting in England, as well as artists, traders, and, crafters.

At the end of the 14th century and the beginning of the 15th century, English kings laid claim on the French throne, thus leading their kingdom into the Hundred Years' War with France. England was strong militarily, and the beginning of the war was going well. It seemed luck was also on its side since the French king, Charles VI, went mad, leaving his country at the brink of a civil war. Henry VI was even crowned as a baby as the king of France, although the title was disputed. However, by 1450 England was once again in crisis. The long war was exhausting, both financially and morally. More social unrest followed, ending with the Wars of the Roses fought between rival lords of England. The end of the Middle Ages started with this war and the victory of Henry VII in 1485.

# Chapter 1 – Roman Province

England under Rome's Control

https://en.wikipedia.org/wiki/Roman_Britain#/media/File:Roman_Britain_410.jpg

As early as 55 BC, the British Islands were of enormous interest to Gaius Julius Caesar, proconsul of Gaul. Two points made Britain extremely interesting to the Romans. For one, they were already trading partners, and much potential money lay in the islands, as they were rich in metal and farmland. Secondly, some of the British tribes had allied themselves with the Gauls of the north that Caesar was already trying to subdue. His visit to the British Isles was imminent, and later, it became an invasion. The first visit wasn't a success for Caesar. He was unaware of the hostility of the tribal leaders, who took the first opportunity to break their vows of peace. He also lost many ships due to unpredictable weather, and he was forced to retreat to Rome. Just a year later, he would come back, this time prepared. A full-scale invasion was in progress, and Caesar brought with him 800 ships, 25,000 infantry units, and 2,000 cavalry units. The British tribes united against the Roman threat and chose one leader to rule them. He was known as Cassivellaunus, king of the territories that lay north of the River Thames.

Caesar had to admit to the bravery and courage the British showed. Their army consisted of infantry, cavalry, and chariotry. British chariots had the purpose of bringing warriors to the front of the battle, then retreating and waiting for the warriors to come back and be taken wherever the battle needed them. Caesar admired the skill of the chariot drivers who could control their horses even when the terrain had extremely steep inclines. The Romans resisted the attacks of the British thanks to their discipline and the iron will of their commanders. After numerous battles, the British started retreating, but Caesar followed. Pursuit was executed with such determination that Cassivellaunus had to capitulate, and his stronghold was destroyed in the process.

Even though Caesar retreated after taking tribute and some prisoners, the slow Romanization of Britain began. The households of the wealthy and the nobles started taking on a Roman rectilinear shape instead of the usual circular shape. Roman goods were imported to the south of Britain, while the war leaders enjoyed Roman wine. Some of the tribal rulers became clients of the rulers of Rome and often sent envoys to Rome to pay a tribute to the emperor. Everyone wanted to imitate the victorious Romans, and the old ways of life started to decline.

But the Romans themselves did not return for nearly a century when, finally, Emperor Claudius decided to attack, as he desired military prestige and glory. The opportunity showed itself when some of the British tribes invited the Romans to help them deal with their hostile neighbors. Instead, Claudius sent two different armies that landed in two separate places in the British Islands, thus confusing the British. These armies consisted of four legions which, in total, numbered around 20,000 men. The British tribes dispersed in front of the Roman army, but they gathered and united for a major battle at Medway (43 AD) in South East England. This battle is one of the most important in English history, but its precise place is not known. It lasted for two days, and the British forces led by Togodumnus and Caratacus were defeated. Claudius himself came with twenty-eight elephants and stormed the capital of Camulodunum (Colchester), declaring victory. However, it took the next forty years to achieve the complete conquest of the British Isles.

The Romans advanced in three directions from Camulodunum, which they declared their new regional capital. Vespasian led the attacks towards Wales and had to fight a total of thirty-three battles before, finally, he captured Somerset so that the Romans could start their mining operations there. The other two operations, in the north and northwest, were led against the tribes. In each major settlement, they built a stronghold and left a small Roman military presence. Roman historians described the colonization of Britain as smooth, but tribal rebellions and mutinies did happen often. It was common to experience raids, ambushes, and small battles everywhere. British tribes were not unified at this time; some fought against the Romans, while others became their allies. Some British tribes waged wars between themselves without any Roman influence.

Britain was militarized under Roman leadership, and the country took a new shape. Permanent fortresses were built at York and Chester, and each housed a Roman legion. Manchester and Newcastle were also built around such forts. The Romans built straight roads linking these forts and ensuring communication between the legions. Lincoln and Gloucester became habitation towns for the retired legionaries. Britain became a vast network of forts, defensive walls, watchtowers, and encampments, all linked by a series of roads. The building process that Rome undertook in Britain did not go as smoothly as expected. Rome taxed the citizens highly and took their grains. It wasn't uncommon to even enslave entire populations to work on these construction projects. Local tribes rebelled under the harsh rule of Rome.

However, the legionaries slowly integrated into British society. First, they were transferred directly from Rome. Later the soldiers were recruited from other conquered areas such as Spain or Germany. In the end, the local populace started joining the legions, and in a few generations, the army became fully localized. The Roman Empire stopped its expanse in the British territories, and to defend themselves from the raids of Britons and Picts, Hadrian's Wall was built. All the lands south of the wall were cultivated, and an extensive agricultural system was developed. Britain became a rich and productive Roman province worthy of investment.

Children of the British elite were often sent to Rome for education, while their parents started dressing in Roman ways to show off their status. They spoke Latin and started building public squares, temples, and other buildings like the Romans did. The new organization of the country under Roman influence affected the government, too. Tribal regions were separated into districts, or *civitates*. The old tribal capitals (oppidum) became centers of *civitates*, and they were rebuilt in stone instead of wood. The government itself was controlled by a council, or *curia*, of major landowners. Each town had its own council and employed clerks and other officials, selecting among educated citizens. The old tribal ties settlements had with each other slowly developed into economically dependent relationships, but this cultural change took place only in cities. Villages were predominantly set in the old customs and religion of the Iron Age. Some of the tribal leaders decided to remain true to the old ways, and they built hill forts in British cultural tradition. British farms also went through gradual but steady changes under Roman influence. Wooden farmhouses were now built out of stone and were often decorated with painted walls. Roman-style bathhouses found their ways onto farms, as well. Barns were first built out of wood, but they too gradually changed to stone. Ovens were used on the farms not just for cooking but also for drying food for livestock. Some bigger farms also employed their own blacksmith or potter. But as for farming, nothing changed, and hadn't since the Bronze or Iron Ages. The Romans did introduce new fruit and vegetables onto British farms, such as figs and cherries, turnips, cabbages, and peas, but unlike the Romans, natives still preferred beef over pork.

By 359, Britain became the breadbasket of Europe with its modernized farms and imperial estates numbering into the hundreds. Some prominent legionnaire generals tried to proclaim themselves emperors of Britain and declare Britain's independence, but Rome did not allow it. Instead, Rome sent armies to retake its prosperous province. Britain reached its peak in prosperity during the 4th century and was a land worth fighting for. Romans ruled Britain for 350 years, but there is much unknown of this period. Historians mostly rely on Roman scripts and texts, which are often biased. The Romans also had the notorious habit of changing the language and Latinizing the names of cities as well as people, making it even more confusing for historians and archeologists to make a precise distinction between British and Roman evidence.

There are also many unknowns in the spread of Christianity throughout Britain. Historians are certain Christianity was introduced some time during the 2nd century. Still, it was a minority religion practiced by small groups of people, and it didn't have much influence on society in the beginning. Latinized British families respected the Roman pantheon, while Iron Age Britons worshiped their own pagan deities. But, an excavation of a Christian cemetery near Dorset dating back to the 3rd century shows that this religion started to spread. Some Christian items were found in Huntingdonshire, near the River Nene. When Constantine the Great was converted to Christianity in 312, this faith became sacerdotal throughout the whole of Britain. Constantine was crowned emperor in York in 306, and he considered Britain one of the religious centers of his empire. He paid three more visits to the province of Britain during his reign. In his honor, London was renamed Augusta at one point. The Romanized population of Britain quickly adapted to Christianity and established faith centers in their cities and towns, where bishops were charged with the conversion of the rest of the population. There are almost no excavation sites of early Christian churches or cathedrals from the 3rd and 4th centuries, but this is because the first sacred places throughout Britain were still considered sacred, and modern churches were being built on the foundation of the old ones. To excavate the old shrines, one would have to destroy existing houses of worship that are still being used today.

At the beginning of the 5th century, a civil war between pretenders to the imperial throne led to Britain suddenly losing Rome's attention. The administration that had pushed the country forward suddenly fell apart. In 408, the northern tribes of Scots and Picts attacked, and the Visigoths were already settled in Aquitania, while the Franks entered northern Gaul. British people had to defend themselves without Rome's help. They managed to fend off barbarian attacks, but they did not stop there. They expelled the Roman governors and started their own administration. But not all British wanted Rome gone. In 410, one group of British nobles asked the Roman emperor to send an army. It is not clear whether they needed help against Saxon raiders or other British groups. Emperor Honorius sent a reply that from then on, Britain had to defend itself. This was the effective end of Roman rule over Britain.

Large landowning families and descendants of old tribal leaders came to power once again and occupied the now abandoned Roman settlements, forts, and villas. Romanized British founded their own kingdoms and continued to work under the familiar Roman administration. These kingdoms often had to rely on mercenaries to defend themselves. The eastern Britain kingdoms used Germanic mercenaries, and this would prove to be a problem later in medieval England.

Since they had no taxes to pay to Rome anymore, the villages and farms were now controlled by an aristocracy of rich landowners. The demand for various products such as pottery did not exist anymore, and many manufacturers were out of business. Villas and other constructions were neglected, and brickmaking did not return to Britain until the 15th century. The cities did not fall into disrepair, however. They changed their function, and the era of public displays was gone. Cities remained major centers of administration and had a bishop and city leader. Many Roman buildings were converted into craft centers, such as for metal or leatherworking. Trade became more localized, and it had to be self-sufficient as all export of goods to the Roman Empire stopped. The commercial population of the cities never left, and they continued to prosper within their walls. The Roman Empire abandoned its province of Britain, but before leaving, it laid the foundation for a future society. Rome's influence stayed present throughout medieval England through its commerce, military, and administration.

Britain was on its own; people had to learn how to live without constant support from Rome. Freshly out of protection, England was an easy target for Saxons, who would invade them later. But this invasion was never as sudden or as overwhelming as history first suggested. Saxons were already in Britain during the early 3rd century. They were part of the British life as employed mercenaries who defended the kingdoms' borders. Many traders living in British cities were Saxons following their military families. They had already spent generations in Britain, as some military families were given lands to work, especially around Kent.

To discern various groups of people who inhabited Britain and are often called British, it is best to give some attention to their proper names. There is common consent to call all Iron Age native British the "Britons." They all spoke Celtic and Gaelic. The native British who lived in the south and east of the country were in the territories inhabited by Saxons, and they gained their name from one of the Saxon settler groups, the Angles, the habitation of which the Vikings later named the "Engla lands." This name became dominant and eventually took its modern form, England.

# Chapter 2 – The Anglo-Saxon Invasion

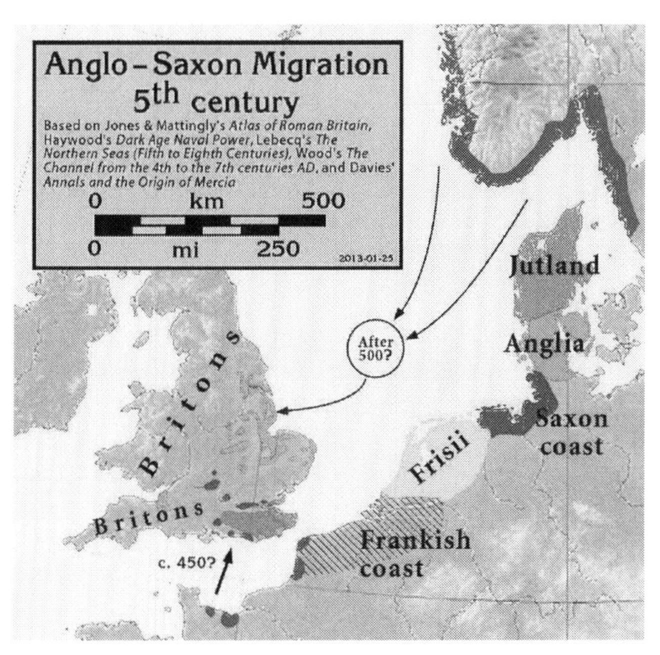


Potential Anglo-Saxon Migration Routes

https://en.wikipedia.org/wiki/Anglo-Saxon_settlement_of_Britain#/media/File:Anglo.Saxon.migration.5th.cen.jpg

The *Anglo-Saxon Chronicle* speaks of mercenaries being sent to Britain to help a certain "Wyrtgeorn" fight the Scottish and Pict invaders. The term "Wyrtgeorn" stands for nothing more than an overlord. It is not a personal name, but there is evidence that the chronicle mentions it in the context of one person. Welsh evidence, for example, speaks of Vortigern "of the repulsive mouth" when mentioning the same events described in the *Anglo-Saxon Chronicle.* Historians have a firm basis to believe Vortigern was a leader of a confederacy of small kingdoms that came into existence after the Roman rule of Britain was over.

Vortigern called Saxon mercenaries to help fight off invaders from Scotland and Ireland. The habit of hiring mercenaries was a legacy of Roman rule, so it was nothing new or unusual for Britain of the early 5th century. Saxon mercenaries were especially known for their valor and ferocity when it came to battle. One of the tactics they used to scare their enemies was to shave the front of their scalp and grow long hair in the back so their faces looked bigger and fiercer. Saxons were mostly stationed in Kent, but they also occupied the Isle of Thanet in the Thames estuary. The sheer numbers of Saxon mercenaries who came to Britain were enough to persuade the invaders to stop the attack and retreat. After the danger of invasion passed, the mercenaries expected to be paid for their troubles.

The allies of Vortigern, seeing the cost of this Saxon army, decided they could not and would not pay. They also refused to give up land in exchange for not paying the armies. The Kentish copy of the *Anglo-Saxon Chronicle* states that the rulers of the kingdom declared they didn't need Saxon help and that the mercenaries should leave without payment, as they could not feed their growing numbers. The mercenaries, who found themselves without food, clothes, or money in Britain, were pushed into an immediate, strong reaction. First, they started revolting in East Anglia, where the insurgency spread to the Thames Valley. Saxons took over some cities and villages, and they established rule in areas which were previously inhabited by them. They seized large estates and enslaved the native Britons who survived their attacks. The territories they took were a prize, rich in cultivated land, and the

Island of Thanet was a granary—in other words, worth conquering. After establishing their rule over the conquered lands, the Saxons sent a call to their homeland for their compatriots to come and settle in Britain, as the natives were easy to subdue.

Germanic tribes of the North Sea kept coming and settling in Britain. Four tribes of these newcomers were predominant: the Angles, whose origins are in Schleswig (Germany), the Saxons from the lands around the river Elbe, the Frisians from the northern shores of the Netherlands, and the Jutes from Denmark. Anglo-Saxons did not exist as a people group until the 6th century when chroniclers needed a single name to unite these settlers. The Jutes occupied Kent, Hampshire, and the Isle of Wight. The Upper Thames valley belonged to the Saxons. The Frisians were scattered all over the southeast of England, but they also had an important part to play in London. The Angles settled the eastern and north-eastern parts of the country. Some of the tribes were welcomed to their settlements and did not have to fight for the right to work the land or to trade in the cities. Others were violently denied access to territories, and they had to wage war. The modern genetic evidence of the population reveals that by the 6th century, Saxons made up only five percent of the population. In some northern regions, this number climbed to ten percent. Evidence suggests that they never tried to replace the whole population of certain regions, and they never committed genocide, even in parts where they had to fight for their right to settle.

Saxons came to England at the time of the great migrations of that era. They were pushed by other tribes and peoples who moved due to climate change. This same climate change threatened to submerge the Saxon lands under sea level.

Vortigern suffered a blow to his authority when the Saxons revolted, and another Romanized British leader, Ambrosius Aurelianus, overthrew him. Ambrosius is a historic figure sometimes described as the last Romanized ruler, but his character develops further in British myths and legends. He is believed to be the uncle of the legendary King Arthur, a brother to Arthur's father, Uther Pendragon. Later, he was even transformed into the great wizard Merlin.

A 6th-century British monk, Gildas the Wise, wrote that Ambrosius was born in a noble house, but his parents were slaughtered in the initial attacks of the Saxons, during the early days of the invasion. He was possibly a Christian, as Gildas writes he won his battles with the help of God, but it could be that the monk's religion influenced his words.

Ambrosius fought the Saxons for ten years, engaging in a series of battles in the attempt to drive them from the coasts of England. In approximately 500 CE, there was a major battle between the native British and the Saxons, known as the Battle of Badon. The details of the battle are unknown, as it is first mentioned in scripts from the 6th century. The battle might be a part of the resistance organized by Ambrosius to repel invading Saxons. The location of the battle, as well as the exact year it happened, is still unknown. Documents from the 6th century and a later one from the 8th century both mention Ambrosius but never directly in relation to the battle itself. There are no names of British or Saxon warlords in any of the surviving texts until the 9th century; it is just an assumption that Ambrosius took part in the battle.

The *Historia Brittonum* from the 9th century is the first document that mentions Arthur related to the Battle of Badon. He is mentioned only as a soldier, not a king, who led the native British, and was to be praised for the victory. The *Historia Brittonum* dates from 828, but its author is unknown. Some historians agree the work should be treated as a compilation of history and myths by various authors, while others believe it was one author who gathered and compiled all the stories. Both the authorship and the origin period of the *Historia Brittonum* are still open for debate among modern historians. Because of the uncertainty that surrounds this text, the information it gives about certain events and people is to be taken with caution.

At approximately the same time as the Battle of Badon, the construction of Wansdyke took place. Wansdyke (from its Saxon name Woden's Dyke) is a series of defensive earthworks consisting of a ditch and a wall. The purpose of these constructions was to separate British-occupied territories from Germanic tribes.

For two or three generations, the Germanic tribes did not mingle with the British people. They were kept separate. But the Plague of Justinian that took many lives in the 540s created an urge for Germanic tribes to move and explore fertile lands that lay in the western parts of the British Isles. The plague started from the Mediterranean and quickly took over the world. It lasted for almost two centuries, and it is estimated to have taken between thirteen and twenty-six percent of the world's population. Later research confirmed that it was *Yersinia pestis* bacterium responsible for the Plague of Justinian, the same bacteria responsible for the later but better-known Black Plague (Black Death) of the 14th century. It is assumed that the plague arrived on the British island due to trade with the Gauls. The English settlements were highly populated and concentrated, which allowed the fast and easy spread of the disease. This may be the reason the plague disproportionally affected various peoples that inhabited Britain, and why native British had a higher death toll than the Germanic tribes. It is presumed that the population of four million Britons dropped to only one million, but there is no firm evidence to reinforce this speculation. The defense of the British lands was sparse, and this gave Angles and Saxons the chance to move westward. The plague did not spare the nobility, either. British kings were deposed, and Anglo-Saxons easily took over the British cities.

The Saxon leader Ceawlin reached Cirencester, eighty miles away from London. By 577, he took over Gloucester and Bath, and only seven years later, he led his forces in the successful conquest of the midlands. Other Saxon warlords were just as successful, and the British population was forced to flee before them. Many remembered tribal ties with the Britons of north-western France and took refuge in these lands, forming Brittany. This migration of people caused mingling among Saxons, Angles, and native British, and these terms ceased to have any meaning. Everyone in the midlands was English now. But in the west, some native rulers kept their lands safe from Saxons for over 200 years. The kingdom of Elmet (West Riding of Yorkshire), for example, survived until the 7$^{th}$ century. Gwynedd, a kingdom in Wales, was captured by English only in 1283. Cornwall still had Celtic speakers until the 6$^{th}$ century, when the language started its decline and officially died during the 18$^{th}$ century.

The settlements of Germanic tribes were small, and each one had territory, usually making a river its natural border. Settlements were made by groups of warriors, and the name of the tribe was turned into the name of the settlement; for example, Haestingas became Hastings. The number of these tribes was significant at first, but gradually, they merged, probably joining forces for warfare or defense of the region. The leaders were overlords who ruled several tribes at once, and whose subordinates were tribal chieftains. By the 600s, the Anglo-Saxon kingdoms of medieval England took their shape and started carving their names into history.

The social structure of the Anglo-Saxon kingdoms included slaves, landless workers, *ceorls* or *churls* (a freeman of the lowest rank), and *thegns* or thanes (owners of land granted by the king, a rank between freeman and noble). Each rank had its own distinction, and the worth of someone's life was measured by his rank. Financial penalties for various crimes differed depending on the rank of both the committer and the victim. Native British people were not exterminated by Saxons, as they remained useful. Artisans and merchants were of high value and were allowed to integrate into the new society and continue their work. They did have to pay taxes or tributes to the local lords. Many of the native British continued working the land–some as slaves, some as freemen–and the Saxons adapted to the British methods of agriculture.

In the north, Germanic tribes were occupying east and south Yorkshire. These territories were known as the Kingdom of Deira. The neighboring Kingdom of Bernicia was established by an Anglian community. Their king, Aethelfrith, was known for ruling both kingdoms by 604. He started his conquest by subduing the Britons. He was so successful that the monks of the 7th century compared him to Saul, the first king of Israel. The monks also noted that he was a pagan, as Christianity entered these territories approximately ten years after Aethelfrith's death. The population of the British territories he conquered were either made tributary states or completely replaced by the English. It is unknown how Aethelfrith came to be the ruler of Deira, but the fact that the son of its previous ruler, Edwin, was exiled, might indicate it was a conquest. But some historians claim that Aethelfrith's rule of both kingdoms was a confirmation of an already existing cooperation agreement between Deira and Bernicia. The exile of Edwin, the rightful successor to Deira's throne, might not have been immediate. It is suggested that the hostility between Aethelfrith and Edwin was gradual and of a later date. Aethelfrith was married to the princess of Deira, Edwin's sister Acha, but it is not known whether he married her prior to becoming the ruler of Deira or after. Between 613 and 616, Aethelfrith defeated the Kingdom of Powys in the Battle of Chester. He also massacred the monks who gathered to help the king of Powys with their prayers. His victory in the Battle of Chester may have influenced the separation of the Welsh Britons from the Britons in the north. Aethelfrith's conquered territories became the Kingdom of Northumbria, and he was its true first king, although, at this time, the kingdom did not bear that name.

After Aethelfrith's death, Edwin came back from exile and became the new king of Northumbria, ruling until his death in 633. Early in his reign, he began an expansion to the west, taking over the Kingdom of Lindsey and conquering the Irish province on the shores of England. Edwin was Christianized during Easter in 626, required to marry the Christian princes of Kent. He even committed to Christianizing his daughter Eanfled, who later became queen of Northumbria. From 627, Edwin was the most powerful ruler among the Anglo-Saxon kingdoms. Besides ruling in Bernicia and Deira, he also became the overlord of the Isle of Man, eastern Mercia, and Anglesey. He was also successful at subduing Wessex and making an alliance with Kent. His power remained unchallenged for a good number of years until his foster brother Cadwallon ap Cadfan joined forces with the Kingdom of Mercia and attacked Edwin in 632/633. Edwin was defeated and killed during this attack. But Cadwallon didn't get to rule his newly conquered lands. Soon after the victory over Edwin, he was attacked by the sons of Aethelfrith, who had returned from their exile in the lands of the Picts. In or right after 642, Edwin's daughter Eanfled married one of the sons of Aethelfrith, Oswiu, and became the queen of Northumbria.

The large lands of East Anglia, or East Angles, also had great kings. Redwald (also spelled Raedwald) was one of them, and he ruled in the 7th century. In fact, he was Edwin's ally and protector during his times in exile. He was the king of East Anglia, which lay in the territories of today's counties of Norfolk and Suffolk. Not much evidence of his reign survived the Viking raid of East Anglia's monasteries during the 9th century. It is believed that he reigned from about 599 until he died in 624. Redwald was directly responsible for making Edwin the king of Northumbria after he fought and killed Aethelfrith. Redwald was the most powerful king ever to rule the southern Anglo-Saxon kingdoms. In the *Anglo-Saxon Chronicle*, he was called a *bretwalda*, which means he ruled over Britain, indicating how powerful he was. Redwald was the first

East Anglian ruler to convert to Christianity in 605, but at the same time, he kept pagan temples alive.

Eminent individuals of the 7th century were usually buried in barrows, or burial mounds, and there is a cemetery at Sutton Hoo in Suffolk, which would be the ideal burial place for Redwald and his family. Unfortunately, Redwald's body was never found, although it is believed he was given a Christian burial. But one mound, discovered in 1993, contains such riches–and even what it was believed to be the scepter of *bretwalda*–that it could be a monument to King Redwald, built as a memorial to his greatness. The mound where this rich burial place was discovered contains an Anglo-Saxon burial ship that was ninety feet in length, filled with riches in coins, jewelry, textiles, and other valuable items. The ship, however, lacks a body and even the shroud ties common for burial practices of the 7th century. The connection between this place and King Redwald is still unproven. Some of the armor found at the site is of Swedish style, which might indicate that the king's ancestors were of Swedish origin. But it also might mean that the tomb belongs to someone else, such as a foreign delegation representative, some aspiring noble, or a prestigious visitor to the kingdom.

The Kingdom of Mercia did not exist as a unified administrative entity in the late 5th and early 6th centuries. The territories occupying the midlands–Essex, Sussex, and Wessex–became the Kingdom of Mercia. It was also the last kingdom to convert to Christianity. Its first known king was Creoda, who came to power in 584. He built a fortress at Tamworth, which would later become the seat of power for all the kings of Mercia to come. But in the *Anglo-Saxon Chronicle*, Creoda wasn't referred to as the king; he was mentioned only as being from West Saxon heritage. Because of this, some historians argue that he did not even exist and that his mentions are probably guesswork derived from other works, such as the one from the English Benedictine monk Bede, who lived during the 8th century.

The Worchester list, another source of historical information, begins counting kings from Penda, who ruled in the 7th century. Penda was still a pagan when Christianity was spreading through the Anglo-Saxon territories like wildfire. It is unknown when Penda became king, or even how. His father, King Pybba, died when Penda was a child. Cearl, a possible relative of Pybba, ruled until approximately 626 CE when Penda became the king of Mercia. The *Anglo-Saxon Chronicle* mentioned that he ruled for about thirty years, but this number is just a guess. Some historians, citing Bede, believe Penda became king only after the defeat and death of Edwin, king of Northumbria, who was the most powerful king of Britain at that time. It is believed that Penda and his ally Cadwallon ap Cadfan, king of Gwynedd, ransacked Northumbria but did not rule over it. Instead, Edwin was succeeded by Oswald, son of Aethelfrith. In the late 620s at Heavenfield, there was a battle between Oswald's army and the allied forces of Cadwallon and Penda. Oswald managed to win this battle and kill Cadwallon. After these events, Oswald regained rule over all Northumbria and forced Penda to recognize his authority. But Penda remained hostile towards Northumbria, and yet another battle, known as the Battle of Maserfield, emerged on August 5, 641/642. Penda, with his Welsh allies, clashed with the forces of King Oswald of Northumbria. It is unknown how this battle started or what caused it, but as Oswald died in the enemy's territory, it is believed he was on the offensive. The result of the battle was an internal weakening of the Northumbrian kingdom as, yet again, Deira and Bernicia chose two separate rulers.

Together with the king of Deira, Penda attacked Bernicia in 655. The cause of this war is unknown, but there are suggestions that the spread of Christianity from Bernicia was seen as an effort to undermine Penda's rule. It is quite possible that Penda started the war to secure his power as an overlord. At this time, the king of Bernicia was Oswiu, who tried even to buy peace with Penda, to no avail. Oswiu won the battle, possibly due to ally Gwynedd's army abandoning Penda at the site of the final battle. Penda was also abandoned by another ally, the kingdom of Deira, which decided to observe the outcome of the battle from a safe distance. The Mercian army was defeated, and Penda was killed.

Penda is famous for being the last pagan warrior-king of the Germanic tribes that invaded England. At the time of his death, paganism ceased to be a public religion and political ideology. Immediately after Penda's death, Mercia became a Christian kingdom, and all three sons of Penda ruled as Christian kings.

Another Anglo-Saxon king, who is mentioned in the *Chronicle* as *bretwalda,* was Aethelbert of Kent. He ruled during the late 6th and early 7^th^ century and was known for allying himself with the Franks by marrying Bertha, daughter of King Charibert of the Franks. At that time, Francia was the most powerful state of contemporary Western Europe. Under its influence, Pope Gregory I sent Augustine as a missionary to Kent to Christianize its king and people.

Aethelbert is credited for the earliest written code in the Germanic language, known as the Law of Aethelbert. The code was written some time in 602 or 603, and it consists of ninety sections. It is no surprise this was the first such document written in Anglo-Saxon since, with Augustine's mission to Christianize people, the literacy era had begun. The laws are heavily influenced by Christian doctrine, and the very first section is about the church and the compensation for a bishop, deacon, and priest, as well as rules for acquiring church property. Furthermore, the code consisted of laws that concern penalties for various crimes, where the severity of punishment depended on the social rank of the involved parties, usually the victim. Most of the punishments were financial, and the king was the one profiting from them. But the king also had the role

of keeping the law and preventing any blood feuds that could arise in the country. Many later kings of other Anglo-Saxon kingdoms wrote their laws based on Aethelbert's code.

# Chapter 3 – Christianity in Anglo-Saxon England

Christianity had been present in Britain since the 3rd century, while Britain was a Roman province. Traders, immigrants, and legionaries who followed Roman expansion probably brought Christianity to the island. There is firm evidence that, by the early 4th century, Britain had organized the Christian community. In 314, three Briton bishops were attending the first Council of Arles, a Christian council in the south of Roman Gaul that followed the legalization of Christianity in the Roman Empire. The names of the three bishops were Eborius of Eboracum (York), Restitutus of Londinium (London), and Adelfius, whose origin remains unknown.

Britain's path towards Christianity started before the Romans abandoned their province. Christianity had nothing to stop it from spreading, and the community grew steadily until the Saxon invasion. After the Romans left, pagans were free to occupy the territories in the southern parts of Britain. In the west, beyond the newly-developed Anglo-Saxon kingdoms, Christians remained. These native British Christians developed their own church, far from the influence of Rome. The most prominent influence came from Irish missionaries. Instead of bishoprics, the native Christians developed monasteries. They calculated Easter differently from Rome, and their hairstyles differed, as they preferred the tonsure (the practice of shaving the scalp as a sign of religious devotion).

During the Anglo-Saxon invasion, Christianity in the east survived, keeping the cult of Saint Alban very much alive. Even though the Saxons often mixed with native British people, no evidence confirms an effort to Christianize the Germanic tribes this early in history.

Pope Gregory I was the first to send a mission to Christianize Anglo-Saxons in Britain. This mission bears the pope's name and is referred to as the "Gregorian Mission." One of the conditions of marriage between King Aethelbert and Princess Bertha of Paris was that she be allowed to continue practicing her Christian religion in Kent, which was pagan at the time. With her, she brought Bishop Liudhard, who restored the Roman church in Canterbury. It is believed that under Bertha's influence, Aethelbert himself asked the pope to send the mission and Christianize his people. Still, some historians believe it was first Pope Gregory's idea since he saw Saxon slaves in Rome's market. The most obvious reason for dispatching a mission was that Kent, under the rule of Aethelbert, became the most powerful kingdom in Britain, and the Christian church wanted to try to influence that power to some extent. In 595, Gregory dispatched the mission, choosing Augustine as its leader. The mission was supported by Frankish bishops and state officials, who not only donated money but also provided translators and priests to accompany Augustine. Gregory chose Augustine for this mission because he was well acquainted with his abilities; Augustine was a monk at the Abbey of Saint Andrew's in Rome, whose abbot was the pope himself. In a letter to King Aethelbert, the pope praised Augustine for his knowledge of the Bible and his administrative abilities.

Augustine had forty companions who, at one point, wanted to abandon the mission and even asked the pope for permission to return to Rome. But Gregory insisted they continue, and finally, in 597, the mission landed in Kent. The monks started preaching in Aethelbert's capital, Canterbury, where they were given the church of Saint Martin's to use for the services. Aethelbert was probably first to convert to Christianity in Kent. Even though there is no mention of the exact date of his conversion, it is commonly believed to be 597. Within just one year, Augustine recorded a large number of conversions. People were willing to accept Christianity since it was the newly-chosen religion of their king.

The king donated land to the first monastery in Kent, the monastery of Saints Peter and Paul, founded by Augustine. Later, this monastery became Saint Augustine's Abbey. It was the first Benedictine abbey outside of Italy, and it is believed that Augustine introduced the Rule of Saint Benedict to England. However, there is no firm evidence that, at the time, the abbey was following this rule. The second mission was dispatched from Rome in 601. The monks brought with them sacred texts, relics, and vestments, and Augustine was made archbishop. Gregory sent a set of rules by which the church in Britain would abide, as well as instructions for Augustine to appoint twelve suffragan bishops and a bishop who would be sent to York. Augustine had instructions to move his seat from Canterbury to London. Still, this move never happened, and there is no knowledge as to why.

In the north of Britain, a version of Christian tradition developed without the influence of Rome, and it is referred to as "Celtic Christianity." After the south and east of the island were under Anglo-Saxon rule, British Christians remained active in the north and west. Around 603, British bishops met Augustine but refused to acknowledge him as archbishop. In 616, Aethelfrith of Bernicia attacked the monks in the Abbey of Bangor-on-Dee because they opposed his rule and gave support to his enemies in prayers. After his death, Aethelfrith was succeeded by Edwin, who was married to a Christian princess of Kent, daughter of Aethelbert. The condition of this marriage was the same as for Aethelbert's marriage to a Frankish princess: for the new queen to be allowed to practice her religion. Edwin and his court became Christians soon after, and even though the country was officially converted, both Bernicia and Deira reverted to paganism after the death of King Edwin.

Oswald of Northumbria became a Christian while in exile in Dal Riata. This kingdom was Gaelic and converted due to Irish missionaries in the mid-6th century. When Oswald returned to Northumbria and took the throne, he asked the abbot of Iona Abbey in Scotland to send a mission that would start Christianizing Northumbria. Bishop Comran was first to try to convert Northumbrians, but his methods proved to be too harsh. He returned to Scotland, claiming that the people of Northumbria were too stubborn to be Christianized. An Irish monk called Aidan was sent as his replacement, as he was first to criticize Comran's methods. Aidan started slowly by building schools, churches, and monasteries in Northumbria. He allied himself with the king and used his help to persuade reluctant people to convert. He was patient in talking to the people and often used the language of the common people to approach them and earn their trust. At first, Aidan did not speak any English, and King Oswald acted as his translator.

In East Anglia, Redwald's stepson Sigeberht was the first king of East Anglia to have converted to Christianity before his succession to the throne. He was in exile when he converted. Becoming a Christian must have allowed Sigeberht to come to power, as he would gain the support of already Christianized allies in Kent and Northumbria. In 631, Felix of Burgundy was sent to East Anglia on a mission, possibly supported by Sigeberht himself, as the two had met in Gaul. Felix founded his episcopal seat at Dommoc, a place lost in history. He also founded a monastery at Soham Abbey. The church in East Anglia followed Roman rules, as Felix himself was greatly influenced by them and was loyal to Canterbury.

Mercia was the last Anglo-Saxon kingdom to accept Christianity. Mercian kings resisted converting until 656 with the reign of King Peada. Though pagans, Mercian kings did not refuse offers of alliance with Christianized Welsh rulers, especially in their efforts against Northumbria. Christianity did exist in Mercia before 656, as its previous king Penda won the Battle of Cirencester (628) and incorporated Christianized West Saxon territories into Mercia. By the mid-7th century when Penda died, Mercia was surrounded by Christian kingdoms and could not resist the conversion any longer. As the only pagan state, Mercia was often excluded from diplomatic and trade deals with other kingdoms, as well as the alliances that demanded dynastic marriages. It was these diplomatic endeavors that brought Christianity to Mercia in the first place. Peada had to marry a princess of Christian Northumbria to gain support from its King Oswiu. The condition for this marriage was that the king of Mercia accept the religion of Princess Alchflaed, daughter of King Oswiu. The first bishop in Mercia was an Irish monk, Diuma, sent by Oswiu himself. To show his devotion to Christianity, Peada founded the abbey at Medeshamstede, today's Peterborough. Even though Peada was Christianized, the rest of his court was reluctant, and there was not much progress in converting the people of Mercia.

Chad, the fifth bishop of Mercia, had the first success in Christianizing the people of this kingdom. Even though his position lasted for only three years, Chad is credited with converting the largest part of Mercia. Sons and successors of Peada were both Christians, and they invested in the Christian mission in Mercia. Wulfhere often donated to the family monastery at Medeshamstede, but he also gave the lands of Lichfield and land at Bawae to Chad, who founded new monasteries there.

The doctrine of the Roman church encouraged strong kings and stable governments. It is not unusual that Anglo-Saxon kings chose Christianity over paganism precisely because of their role in the country. Kings were declared saints even in life, and their role within the church meant a stronger grip over the country. Religious people were also easier to control, especially when they were convinced that the king was chosen by God himself. The majority of the literate members of society were the priests, and it was inevitable that they would be appointed as administrators of the state. Thus, the church entered the domain of statesmanship and gained control over all aspects of political affairs.

Eventually, Christianity managed to unite the kingdom. Under the same God, various smaller kingdoms started uniting and becoming one. The church became one, and it demanded one country; it demanded that all the people be under a single ruler. Early historians such as the monk Bede excluded the Welsh and the Picts from the united Church of England, creating the image of England as we know it today.

# Chapter 4 – Viking Attacks

The expansion of the Vikings

https://en.wikipedia.org/wiki/Viking_expansion#/media/File:Viking_Expansion.svg

During the late 8th century, Christian monasteries in the British islands came under attack by a new pagan enemy. In the final stages of the Iron Age, Scandinavia was still a pre-literate society trying to find its place in the world of rapid technological and economic development. For Scandinavia, the end of the century meant the beginning of what historians call the "Viking Age." The reasons Vikings indulged in nautical raids are unknown, but there are three main theories. Norway lacked land suitable for farming, and it is possible that the Vikings first set off for other countries in hopes of finding farmable land. Upon seeing Christian monasteries and their non-existent defenses, the Scandinavians decided to raid them. The second reason might be the "youth bulge effect," in which the eldest son is the one who would inherit the family estate, leaving the younger sons to find their own fortune. Many young men turned to exploring and adventuring in the hope of gaining riches. The third possible reason was the lack of women for reproduction. Vikings might have practiced the selection of their offspring, in which undesired daughters would be killed. If this were the case, Scandinavians would have to search for their wives in other countries. There is no conclusive evidence for any of the theories as to why the Scandinavians started raiding on the shores of the British Isles. Still, once they did, the monasteries, filled with gold and silver relics as well as food, were their primary target.

The first monasteries the Vikings encountered and attacked were situated on little islands around the British coast. Monks sought isolation to be able to devote their lives to God undisturbed. On these islands, the monasteries were too far away from any defense or help that could come and save them from Viking pillaging. The Scandinavians were shocked to learn of communities that carried no weapons to protect themselves but housed such riches. These attacks were the first contact Vikings had with Christianity, but the attacks were not religious. They saw monasteries as easy targets, and they did not care what their purpose was.

The first recorded Viking raid happened in 787 when three ships from Norway landed on the territory of southern Wessex, on the Isle of Portland. Scandinavians were greeted by the local officials from Dorchester, who mistook them for traders and whose task was to identify all new merchants who landed on this part of the British islands. The Scandinavian party killed them all. Other raids possibly happened, but there were no surviving records to offer evidence. In 792, King Offa of Mercia prepared to defend Kent from the pagans who attacked it. The next year, a monastery on the eastern coast, at

Lindisfarne, was attacked. The records survived through history and even offer the exact date of the attack: June 8, 793. The chronicler described the cruelty of the Vikings, mentioning that the monks were not just simply cut down with swords; they were also purposely drowned or taken away as slaves. Lindisfarne endured numerous Viking raids—it was pillaged for nearly eight decades—just to be abandoned in 875.

In 795, Iona Abbey, on an island off Scotland's west shore, was raided. This abbey suffered more attacks, two of which were recorded in 802 and 806. The last one was so devastating that the monks decided to finally abandon this site.

One of the last Viking raids to happen for the next forty years was an attack on a rich monastery at Jarrow in 794. Finally, the Vikings encountered some resistance in which the British managed to kill all their leaders. The Viking raiders started retreating but found their ship beached at Tynemouth. Their whole crew was killed. Intimidated by this event, the Vikings began raiding the coasts of Scotland and Ireland for the time being.

In 865, a "Great Heathen Army" of Danish Vikings landed in East Anglia. Previously uncoordinated bands of raiders were now united under the leadership of two brothers known as Ivar the Boneless and Halfdan Ragnarsson. The brothers were sons of the famous Norse Viking hero and king, Ragnar Lothbrok, of whom many northern sagas tell stories. Some historians believe that attacks led by the Viking brothers were retaliation for Ragnar's death, who, it is believed, died in Britain where King Aelle of Northumbria cast him into a pit filled with snakes. Ivar the Boneless made peace with the king of East Anglia. Ivar promised he wouldn't raid the king's lands if he provided an army with horses. In 867, upon receiving what was promised, Ivar led his army to Northumbria, where they attacked and conquered its capital, York. Defeating both King Osberht and the later usurper, Aelle, the Danes chose Ecgberht I of

Northumbria to be their puppet ruler. The rule of Ecgberht I is scarcely recorded, and little is known of him.

The same year, the Viking army moved south and attacked the kingdom of Mercia. Conquering Nottingham, Vikings decided to spend the winter in this town. King Burgred of Mercia allied himself with King Ethelred of Wessex. Together, they tried to regain Nottingham by laying siege to the town, but they were unsuccessful since the Danes refused to face them in an open battle. When the winter was over, the Viking leader Ivar agreed to a truce in which he agreed to lead his army back to York. The Vikings spent the next year in the city of York planning further attacks.

Once again, Ivar turned to East Anglia, but this time to conquer it. The Vikings defeated King Edmund of East Anglia, who remained known in history as Edmund the Martyr, in 869. King Ethelred of Wessex and his brother Alfred tried to stop the Danes and attacked their army at Reading, but they were unsuccessful and suffered heavy losses. Halfdan, who was now in charge of the Great Heathen Army, decided to pursue the Anglo-Saxon king, and on January 8, 871, the armies clashed at the Battle of Ashdown, where Ethelred and Alfred were victorious. To achieve this victory, King Ethelred divided his army and stationed it on each side of the ridgeway. He personally commanded one part of the army while Prince Alfred commanded the second part. Alfred did not wait for the command of his king to attack and ordered his troops to charge. He managed to defeat the Vikings, who also had to split their army in two. Ethelred, though late with his attack, was also victorious in leading the other half of the Saxon army. It is believed that the Saxons had a slight advantage with their numbers, but the Danes were the ones holding the high ground. Meeting the resolve of the two brothers, Halfdan decided to be cautious and chose easier battles during their future raids into the territory of Wessex. After the Battle of Ashdown, the Danes retreated to Basing, where they gained reinforcements. Ethelred followed and attacked, but he was defeated and forced to retreat. The Danes had one more victory over the Wessex king at the Battle of Meretum in March of the same year.

King Ethelred died on April 23, 871, and Alfred succeeded him on the throne of Wessex. To keep the peace with the Danes, Alfred had to pay tribute to Halfdan, who, in turn, left Wessex and attacked Mercia. The Danish campaign in Mercia lasted until 874, after which the command over the Danish army now belonged to Guthrum, who managed to finish the campaign in Mercia. By 876, the Danes conquered the territories of Mercia, Northumbria, and East Anglia. Wessex was the only kingdom still resisting.

The first conflict between Guthrum and Alfred happened on the south coast of Wessex when Guthrum's forces joined another Viking army that was busy fighting in the area between Frome and Piddle rivers. The Danes won the first battle, capturing one small tower and a convent of nuns. Alfred negotiated a peace that was broken by Guthrum the very next year. The Danish and Wessex armies confronted each other in various skirmishes, and Guthrum was victorious in all of them. The Danish army left Wessex to spend the winter in Gloucester after agreeing to Alfred's second attempt at peace.

On Epiphany day (January 6) in 878, while Alfred's Christian kingdom celebrated and enjoyed the festivities, Guthrum launched a surprise attack on the court of Wessex at Chippenham, Wiltshire. The Saxons were unaware of the attack, but Alfred managed to escape and took refuge in the marshes of Somerset, in a small village called Athelney. He stayed in the village for a few months and used it as a base to launch guerilla attacks on the Danes. Soon after, he called all loyal Englishmen to join him at the supposed site of Egbert's Stone, where they began their march to Edington to confront the Danish invaders.

In 878, the clash between Danes and Saxons at the Battle of Edington would end Guthrum's hopes of conquering Wessex. The exact day of the battle is not known, but historians assume it happened somewhere between May 6 and 12. Alfred applied Viking tactics and trained his army to form a shield wall. They held the position for a very long time, and the Danes broke their ranks. The Danes were forced to retreat, and they took refuge in a fortress, although it is not known which one. The army of Wessex removed all sources of food Danes would use to survive the siege, and, after only two weeks, the Danes were the ones asking for peace. But the Vikings were known for breaking the peace, and Alfred needed a confirmation that this time, they would leave Wessex. In addition to all the usual peace treaty clauses, Guthrum promised to accept baptism and become a Christian.

There are a few reasons why Alfred managed to defeat Guthrum easily. First is the size of his army, as Guthrum had lost the support of other Danish leaders such as Halfdan and Ubba. In addition, Guthrum lost a total of 120 ships, together with their crews, due to storms in 876 and 877. Finally, during the attack on Wessex, the Danes experienced disunity among their ranks, and, instead of spending time to resolve the internal disputes, Guthrum led them into another attack.

Guthrum was baptized and converted to Christianity three weeks after the Battle of Edington. Alfred was his sponsor (equivalent to today's godfather), and the ceremony took place at Aller in Somerset. His Christian name was Athelstan. Many historians speculate that Alfred wanted to bind Guthrum to the Christian ethical code with this baptism, ensuring the Danes wouldn't break any future peace treaties. Guthrum retreated with his army to East Anglia, where he ruled as a king until his death in 890. Although his rule was not completely peaceful, Guthrum was never again a threat to Alfred and Wessex. Alfred fought other Viking armies under different leaders with much more success as he established a system of fortified cities, known as burhs, an Old English word from which the English word borough is derived.

Following the Battle of Edington, a set of legal terms and definitions were created to manage the treaty between Alfred and Guthrum. Known as Danelaw, it meant that people under Danish rule had to obey Danish law. In the 11th century, this term expanded and was given a geographical designation. Territories ruled by Danes were then referred to as Danelaw. They were comprised of fifteen shires: Leicester, York, Nottingham, Derby, Lincoln, Essex, Cambridge, Suffolk, Norfolk, Northampton, Huntington, Bedford, Hertford, Middlesex, and Buckingham. The Danish leaders in England organized an intense process for the settlement of Danelaw: they brought new people from northwestern Europe to settle and live their lives in England. Danish farmland was situated around a fortified town, which was the assembly point for the population of that region. It also served as a defense point since the Danish army inhabited it. The language of these territories changed under the new Danish influence. A new dialect emerged, and it was a mixture of Anglo-Saxon and Norse languages. Many modern English towns still carry a name of Danish or Norwegian origin, such as Whitby or Thurgarton. The survival of British or Saxon names in the territories of Danelaw suggests that the new Viking settlers left the old population alone and assimilated them instead of expelling them. It is possible that because Saxons and Danish people shared a common culture in their old faith, it was easy for them to integrate and mingle.

Danelaw areas started flourishing in trade, and they became prosperous lands. The three wealthiest shires during the 11th century were Norfolk, Suffolk, and Lincolnshire, all three belonging to Danelaw. York became one of the richest cities in England, housing various crafters and traders. Trade was opened with Scandinavia, but also with France and Ireland. Mostly Danes traded in fish, salt, and slaves, as well as wine and pepper.

Edward the Elder succeeded his father, Alfred the Great, and together with his sister, Aethelflaed, Lady of the Mercians, he conquered the Danish territories in Northumbria and East Anglia. This feat was achieved through a series of campaigns they put together in 910. The Danish lords (Jarls) who submitted to them were allowed to keep their lands. To keep their lands safe from further Viking attacks, Edward and Aethelflaed started constructing fortresses in all the conquered territories. The fort at Hertford, which protected London, convinced the British people who lived under Danish rule to submit to Edward. After Aethelflaed's death in 918, Aelfwynn, Aethelflaed's daughter, ruled for a few months until Edward removed Aelfwynn from the throne and carried her back to Wessex. Afterward, Edward united the newly conquered East Anglia with Wessex and Mercia.

It took three generations to Christianize the people who inhabited Danelaw, but some of the territories survived in their northern culture. Orkney and the Shetlands kept their Viking identity until the late 15th century when they were surrendered to Scotland. In the Shetlands, the Norwegian language could be heard among inhabitants until the late 18th century.

Edward was succeeded by his son Athelstan, whose name means "noble stone" in Old Norse. He ruled from 924 to 927 as king of the Anglo-Saxons. Athelstan is also known as the first king of England, ruling as such from 927 until 939. Edward the Elder had conquered all Danish territories in East Anglia and Mercia, but the kingdom of York still thrived under Danish ruler Sihtric (or Sitric). Athelstan married his sister to this Danish king. In doing so, they made a pact never to attack one another and never to ally to each other's enemies. However, Sihtric died the next year, and Athelstan took the opportunity to invade and conquer York. The northern kings accepted him as their overlord, and seven years of peace followed.

Athelstan was linked by marriage to Aquitaine, a French province, as well as with the empire of Germany. His court was always inhabited by poets and scholars who worked tirelessly in gathering knowledge. Athelstan established a coinage that would become valid through all of England, and he had all the control over trade within the kingdom. The oldest surviving English royal portrait depicts Athelstan wearing a crown in the company of Saint Cuthbert.

A new wave of Viking attacks started in 947, with York falling to the armies of the Norwegian king, Eric Haraldsson, nicknamed Eric Bloodaxe. At that time, Northumbria was the main point of conflict between Anglo-Saxons and Vikings. In 946, Eadred, son of Edward, became the English ruler, and he managed to regain control of Northumbria while at the same time gaining control of his allies, the Scots. He also met with Archbishop Wulfstan and the Northumbrian witan (Anglo-Saxon council or parliament), which then pledged its obedience to him. But Northumbrians didn't want English rule and quickly showed their disobedience by electing Eric as their king. Angered, Eadred launched a retaliatory raid on Northumbria, during which Ripon Cathedral was burned. The attack had the desired effect as, soon, Northumbrians renounced Eric as their king to appease the English ruler. But peace didn't arrive in Northumbria. The very next year, 948, Malcolm I of Scotland attacked and raided its territories as far as the River Tees. Eadred did not take any action towards Northumbria, or so the lack of evidence in surviving texts suggests. Northumbria was now under the rule of King Olaf, but the people expelled this king and again swore allegiance to Eric. However, his second rule was just as short. In 954, they expelled him as well.

## England under the Danes

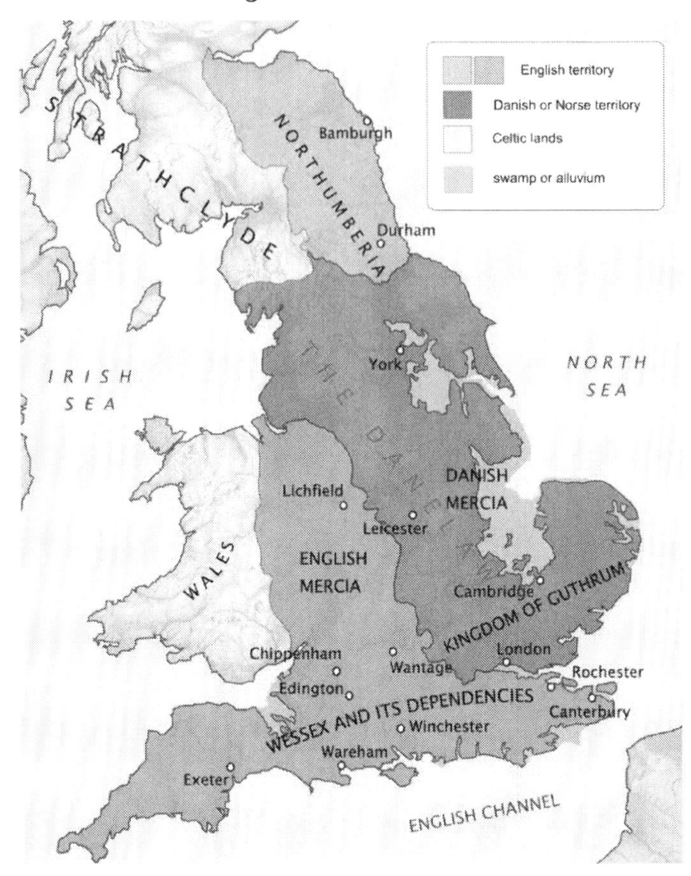


England in 878, the Danelaw in red

https://en.wikipedia.org/wiki/Viking_expansion#/media/File:England_878.svg

Viking attacks and rule over territories in England continued with the rule of King Cnut the Great. He was elected as king by the Vikings, who lived under Danelaw, and only then did he come into the light of history. But his rule was brief. Shortly after, he was forced to flee to Denmark when Ethelred (or Aethelred) II, also known as Ethelred the Unready, came back from Normandy and claimed England. In Denmark, Cnut met with his brother King Harald, who offered the command of his army to Cnut for another invasion of England. Cnut assembled a large fleet and even had help from some Polish troops, as he was related to the Duke of Poland,

Boleslaw I the Brave. Other cousins, therefore allies, were the Swedish successor to the throne and Trondejarl, the co-ruler of Norway. Commanding a fleet of 200 longships, Cnut launched an invasion of England in 1015. Various battles were fought over the next fourteen months, mostly against Edmund Ironside, the eldest son of King Ethelred II. The Earl of Mercia abandoned Ethelred and, taking his forty ships, joined Cnut. Wessex submitted to the Vikings in late 1015.

The next year, Cnut led his army north, crossing the Thames and devastating eastern Mercia. Prince Edmund tried to stop the Viking advance, but he too was abandoned by the ally Uhtred, the Earl of Northumbria, who submitted to Cnut after his forces were devastated. Edmund had no choice but to retreat to London, where he remained undefeated behind the city walls and was crowned king after the death of Ethelred.

Hearing word that Cnut had turned south and was leading his army to London, Edward abandoned the city and went to Wessex, where he hoped to gather an army. But Cnut divided his forces and sent one part after Edward while using the second part to besiege London. The Danish army built dikes on the northern and southern sides of the city, where they also dug a channel connecting the northern part of the Thames with its southern part, encircling the city of London. Longships were placed in this channel to cut communication by river with the territories beyond London.

Edmund crossed the Thames at Brentford with his army and temporarily freed London of the Danish siege. But his army suffered great losses, and he was again forced to retreat to Wessex. The Danes were free to besiege London once again. But this siege was also short-lived, as the Danes were attacked by the English, who managed to defeat Cnut's army and force it to retreat to Kent. Instead of again trying to conquer London, Cnut satisfied himself with leading his army in raids over Mercia. He targeted Mercia because its earl, Eadric Streona, chose to side with Edward in the effort to drive the Danes out of England.

In 1016, a decisive battle between Edmund's and Cnut's forces took place, possibly near Ashingdon or Ashdon. The location is unknown, but the confrontation of the armies of England and the Danes is remembered as the Battle of Assandun. It is unknown if Eadric Streona again changed his allegiance, or his alliance with Edmund was just a ruse, but he decided to retreat from the battlefield. This decision led to the defeat of Edmund and the English forces. Edmund fled with a small contingency of his army but was pursued by Cnut. He was caught in Gloucestershire, where he met his Welsh allies. There, another battle was fought, probably near the forest of Dean. Wounded, Edmund agreed to negotiations and accepted the terms: the region of England north of the Thames was to become Danish domain, while the English king kept the southern parts, including London. But all of England was to be passed to Cnut upon Edmund's death. Edmund died only a few weeks after the conclusion of the peace treaty. Many historians speculate he was murdered, but the circumstances of his death remain unknown. Saxons had to accept Cnut as their king, and he was officially crowned by Lyfing, Archbishop of Canterbury in London in 1017, thus becoming king of England.

As the king of England, Cnut ruled for almost two decades, providing protection from Viking raids. In return for that protection, English allies helped him to recover control of his homeland territories in Scandinavia. However, the first year of his rule was marked by the executions of English noblemen intended to eliminate any challenge to the throne by surviving members of the previous Wessex dynasty. Some princes managed to find protection among their foreign relatives. For example, Ethelred's sons by Emma of Normandy fled to the Duchy of Normandy, where they found refuge. Emma stayed in England, and she was wed to Cnut in

July of 1017. The royal pair had a son, Harthacnut, who was proclaimed an heir to Cnut.

By 1018, Cnut managed to pay off his Viking army and sent them home, except for forty longships and their crews, which stayed in England as his standing army. To reward the Scandinavians who served him, he collected an annual army tax called heregeld. This tax had been established in 1012 by King Ethelred.

Cnut continued governing the kingdom of England by dividing it into shires that would be grouped under the rule of a single ealdorman. The country was divided into four administrative regions, each having its own earl. Earl was a Scandinavian title that was used instead of the English title ealdorman. Cnut, as king of England, by tradition kept Wessex under his personal rule while giving Northumbria to Erik of Hlathir and East Anglia to Thorkell the Tall. Mercia remained under Eadric Streona. All earldoms initially fell under the rule of Scandinavian rulers, but this favoritism was short-lived. As some of the Anglo-Saxon families proved their loyalty to Cnut, he granted them earldom over these territories. The previous Scandinavian rulers either died or fell into disfavor with the king. Cnut eventually gave up on ruling Wessex by himself and handed control of it over to Godwin, an Englishmen from a noble family. This system of dividing the country into shires and then grouping them as administrative units wasn't Cnut's idea. It was a system set by the first king of England, Athelstan, back in 927.

In 1019, Cnut ascended to the Danish throne as he succeeded his brother, Harald II. However, his commitment to England was strong. By 1020, he went back to leaving Denmark in the hands of a regent. As a king who was not in his own country, Cnut's rule was opposed by the Danish people. Instead, they chose his son, who was still a child but present in Denmark, as their king. Cnut had to go back and deal with the situation, but while restoring himself as king of Denmark, he was attacked by an alliance of Norway and Sweden. Successfully defeating them, Cnut became a dominant ruler in Scandinavia. In an official letter to his subjects, dating from 1027, Cnut proclaimed himself king of England, Denmark, Norway, and part of Sweden.

Cnut ruled as a Christian king; his baptism name was Lambert. He even visited Rome in 1027. The occasion was the coronation ceremony of Holy Roman Emperor Conrad II, but Cnut took the opportunity to negotiate with the pope for lower taxes on pallium for English archbishops. He also successfully negotiated improved conditions for pilgrims and merchants who were on their way to Rome from the kingdoms he ruled.

Although Christian, Cnut conflicted with the church on more than one occasion. His ruthless execution of the successors to the Wessex dynasty did not grant him any favors with the church. The fact that he had an open relationship with his concubine, Aelfgifu of Northampton, while he was officially married to Emma of Normandy, led him to clash with the church. To appease the religious leaders of his kingdom, as well as his guilt, Cnut repaired all churches and monasteries in England that had suffered from the Viking attacks. In addition, he donated wealth to Christian religious leaders and monastic communities. Christianity was new and on the rise in Denmark during the time of Cnut's rule, and his sister Estrid was the patron of the first church built in Denmark. Evidence in poetry that surrounds the image of King Cnut suggests he was also fond of pagans. Because of this, historians are not sure if he was deeply devoted to Christianity or used the religion as a tool to reinforce his rule over the Christianized people of England. He often gifted land and even tax exemptions to monasteries and churches, but churches were not the only entities to enjoy his gifts. He often sent relics, religious books engraved in gold, and donations in coins to his neighbors as a sign of their common desire for a Europe unified in the Christian faith.

After Cnut's death in 1035, the kingdoms he ruled were once again divided. England did not accept the new Danish king,

Harthacnut, as its ruler because he spent too much time in Denmark. However, in 1040, he managed to bring the crowns of Denmark and England together once again—but only for the next two years. Edward the Confessor came back from his exile in Normandy and made a treaty with Harthacnut, which stated that if Harthacnut did not have male successors to the English throne, the crown would go to Edward. Harthacnut died in 1042, and Edward became king, bringing the Norman influence to England that would pave the path for the invasion in 1066 by William the Conqueror.

# Chapter 5 – Norman Invasion

Depiction of the Normans landing in England

https://en.wikipedia.org/wiki/Norman_conquest_of_England#/media/File:Bayeux TapestryScene39.jpg

While Edward the Elder and his sister campaigned in England to retrieve the territories conquered by the Danes, in France, a Viking was being named the first ruler of Normandy. In 911, Vikings got permission to settle in Normandy, the northern part of France, as part of the Treaty of Saint-Clair-sur-Epte, signed between their leader Rollo and the French king, Charles the Simple.

As the first mentions of Rollo are in historical texts that describe the siege of Paris from 885 to 886, no evidence confirms his origin. Different sources claim he was of Danish, Norwegian, and Swedish descent, but none of these sources are from his lifetime. His biographers mention his friendship with the English king Alstem, whom historians recognize as Guthrum, a Danish king who took the name Athelstan after being baptized.

Rollo persuaded Charles the Simple that he and his Viking companions would be good allies to the Franks. In exchange for protection from further Viking raids, Charles granted him the lands between the mouth of the Seine River and the city of Rouen. Rollo was baptized and was supposed to marry Gisela, daughter of King Charles. There is no evidence of this marriage taking place, which might suggest either that she was his illegitimate daughter or that she never existed.

The Viking settlers in France formed a new political entity. They were Norsemen, but, in French, this word took a slightly different form: Normans. The Vikings living in France adapted to the culture. They spoke French, they were Christianized, and they married French women. They were creating a new identity for themselves, and they were creating Normandy. Slowly, they expanded their territories and even gained Brittany. It took only a few generations for Franks and Normans to achieve convergence, but the Normans were always known as a society of the most disciplined warriors in Europe.

English king Ethelred the Unready married Norman princess Emma of Normandy in 1002. Their son, Edward the Confessor, spent many years in exile in the court of his mother's family in Normandy, forced to flee before the Viking invasions. He returned to England when Harthacnut invited him to be his heir, where he took the throne and started ruling in 1042. He was a king influenced by Norman politics, and he worked for Norman interests in England. He brought Norman clerics, courtiers, and even soldiers to support him in his rule of England since he felt closer to his mother's origins after spending nearly twenty-eight years in Normandy. Some historians even argue that it was Edward who started the Norman invasion of England. Upon his coronation in 1043, three Norman clerics were given bishoprics in England.

Edward also brought powerful people from Normandy who started building castles instead of Saxon halls. He granted Sussex ports to Normandy's Fécamp Abby and even a part of London's port to traders from Rouen.

When Edward died, leaving no apparent heir, the struggle for the English throne began. Officially, Harold Godwinson of Wessex was crowned king, but Duke William of Normandy claimed that Edward promised him the crown upon his death and that Harold was present and swore on sacred relics that he would bow to William. A similar claim came from the king of Norway, Harald Hardrada, who said the English throne was promised to him by Edward's predecessor King Harthacnut. Both William of Normandy and Harald of Norway prepared their armies to invade England.

Harald Hardrada gathered 300 ships for his invasion and landed on northern English soil in September 1066. At that time, English King Harold and his army were in the south, awaiting the invasion from William of Normandy. It took them some time to turn north and meet the Norwegian army to defend England from invasion. At the Battle of Stamford Bridge, Harold managed to surprise the Norwegians and win the battle. King Harald Hardrada was killed, and Norway suffered such losses that they needed only twenty-four ships of the initial 300 to carry the survivors home. Harold Godwinson may have been victorious, but his army, too, was weakened after the Norwegian attack, and he had yet to face William of Normandy.

## William the Conqueror

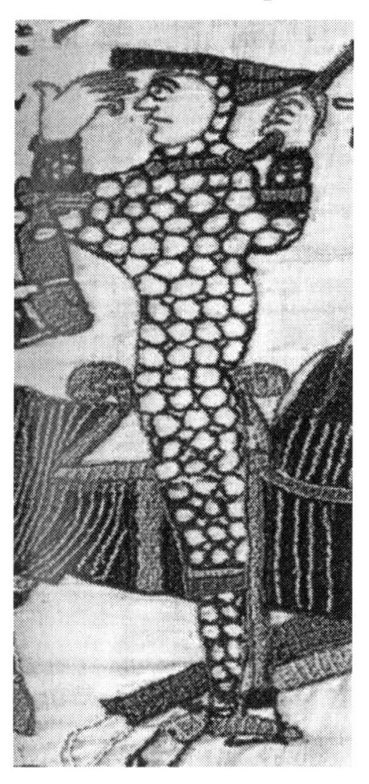

William the Conqueror depicted on the Bayeux Tapestry

https://en.wikipedia.org/wiki/William_the_Conqueror#/media/File:Bayeuxtapestr yilliamliftshishelm.jpg

William of Normandy was the illegitimate son of Robert I and Herleva, the daughter of a tanner. She was probably a member of the Duke of Normandy's household, but she never officially married Robert. William was born in 1027 or 1028; the exact date is unknown. Robert appointed William as his heir and even convinced his noblemen to swear loyalty to William. Robert left for a pilgrimage to Jerusalem, and he died in Nicea on his way back to Normandy in 1035. William did face some challenges upon becoming a Duke of Normandy. He was too young and an illegitimate son. The surviving written evidence suggests he was only seven or eight years old when Robert died. But he did have the support of his great-uncle Robert, who was an archbishop, and of the King of France, Henry I.

Archbishop Robert died in 1037, leaving William with only one remaining supporter. Normandy fell into anarchy that lasted for ten years. There were many attempts to assassinate the young duke, and he had to change guardians several times during his childhood. Some were killed while on duty; others, in fear for their lives, had to abandon William. Often, he had to hide in the houses of peasants to avoid being murdered. Three cousins protected William and would later enjoy his gratitude and become an important influence on his career: William FitzOsbern, Roger de Beaumont, and Roger de Montgomery. Young William continued to have the support of King Henry I, but this support couldn't stop the open rebellion in lower Normandy in 1046. The goal of the rebellion was to capture William, but he managed to escape, and King Henry gave him refuge. Together, they returned to Normandy in 1047, where they won the Battle of Val-ès-Dunes against rebels whose leader was Guy of Burgundy—a man with a claim on the Duchy of Normandy. William assumed Guy's titles and power in Normandy. To limit the violence throughout his duchy, he promoted "Truce of God," a law that prohibited fighting on certain days (such as Sunday and festive days).

Although William regained his position of power in Normandy, he still had to fight the nobility who were against him. First, he followed Guy of Burgundy, who had retreated to his castle at Brionne. After besieging him, William managed to defeat Guy and exile him in 1050. With the help of King Henry, William managed to secure the Bellême family estates, which were strategically positioned to secure their independence from three French overlords. But King Henry didn't like the constantly-growing power of William and his duchy. He also wanted to retain his dominance over Normandy, which was growing independent very fast. King Henry joined forces with Geoffrey II, called Martel, count of Anjou, and decided to attack William. At the same time, nobles in Normandy were again rebelling against William's rule. In 1054, King Henry launched an attack on Normandy at the same time the rebellion was taking place. William was forced to divide his forces and wage war on two fronts. William's supporters helped him easily defeat the rebels, but his dispute with the king of France continued until 1060, when Henry died, and the power shifted completely to William. William did have the help of one of the most powerful French territories, Flanders. He was married to Matilda of Flanders, daughter of Count Baldwin V of Flanders, in 1049 or 1050. This marriage bolstered William's power, and he had four sons and six daughters with Matilda.

William was often described as a strong man with plenty of stamina. It is said he had no rival in archery or in horse riding. Although there was no official portrait of him completed while he was alive, examinations of his femur show that he was approximately five feet and ten inches tall. He was blessed with good health until old age, but he gained a lot of weight in his mature years. William was a descendant of Rollo, a true Norseman. As such, he was schooled in warfare. He won his first battle when he was only nineteen, and he was ruthless. He could command and bend people to his will; he was a true leader with power over Normandy, a warrior society.

The *Anglo-Saxon Chronicle* claims that William visited England once, in 1051, and this might be the year when King Edward promised him the crown. However, such a trip is unlikely since, at that time, William was occupied fighting the count of Anjou.

## The Battle of Hastings

Portrayal of the Battle of Hastings

https://en.wikipedia.org/wiki/Battle_of_Hastings#/media/File:Bayeux_Tapestry_scene57_Harold_death.jpg

William gathered a large army, including soldiers from not just Normandy, but all over France. He had the help of men from Brittany, as well as contingents of Flanders. The force rallied at Saint-Valery-sur-Somme and waited for the building of the fleet to be finished. History doesn't detail the exact number of William's army, although modern researches estimate this number to be anywhere between 7,000 and 12,000 men. Some enthusiasts would go as far as to claim that William had an army of 150,000, but that number is greatly inflated. The number of ships that transported the army to England is also unknown, but the fleet was ready at the beginning of August. However, William decided to wait. It might have been the winds that were not suitable for sailing or intelligence from England notifying him of the position of King Harold's army that made him wait. One thing is certain: Harold moved his army to face the invasion from Norway, which gave William the opportunity for an undisturbed landing on English territory.

After Harold's victory over the Norwegians on September 25, William crossed the English Channel and landed in Sussex on September 28. Immediately after landing, William ordered the construction of a wooden castle at Hastings. This castle served as a base from which the Normans often raided surrounding areas. The raids not only supplied the Norman army but also served the purpose of antagonizing Harold and ensuring he was the first to attack, to stop the raids. Lands around Hastings were the property of Harold's family and should have fed the English army, not the Normans.

To secure the northern parts of his kingdom, Harold was forced to leave a large portion of his army there. He started a march towards the south with the rest of the army, and it was on this march he learned that William had already landed in Sussex. To strengthen his forces, Harold had to spend a week in London before going to meet William. He also hoped that the slight delay would give him the advantage and that he would catch William by surprise, but Norman scouts always knew the exact position of the English army. William decided to lead his army and meet Harold out in the open. Harold, on the other hand, took up a defensive position on Senlac Hill, which was only six miles (ten km) away from Hastings.

As with William's army, the size of Harold's army is unknown. Norman sources claim the number was between 400,000 and 1.2 million, which is an obvious exaggeration for the purpose of propaganda. Historians estimate the real number did not exceed 13,000. More likely, the army consisted of anywhere between 7,000 and 8,000 English men. The English army consisted of *fyrds*, a group of selected representatives (mostly villagers) from self-sustaining households who were obliged to serve the army, and housecarls, which were troops in personal service to someone, equal to nobles or kings' bodyguards. The *fyrds* and armies of housecarls both fought on foot, but the main difference was in their armor. The English army also had *thegns*, the local elites, or nobles who owned land. They usually fought next to housecarls. Although there is evidence that Edward the Confessor, influenced by Norman heritage, built castles that served as training centers for cavalry, the

English army didn't use them with great success. There are no records of cavalry in King Harold's army that fought at Hastings.

The main difference between the Norman and English armies was a lack of archers on the English side. The Norman army consisted of infantry, cavalry, and archers. The main armor was chainmail hauberk, with scales of metal or hardened leather attached to them. On their heads, soldiers usually wore metal helmets with prolonged metal pieces to protect their noses. Infantry shields were round and made of wood reinforced by metal. Horsemen had kite-shaped shields, and some of them were equipped with lances. The swords used by both infantry and cavalry were long, straight, and double-edged. Some soldiers may have used maces instead of swords, and infantry also had long spears. Most of the archers didn't have any special armor, and they used either simple bows or crossbows.

There are many accounts of the Battle of Hastings, but they contradict each other, and it is impossible to construct a precise description of the battle. One fact that all historical records agree on is that the battle started at 9 a.m. on Saturday, October 14, 1066. The records also agree that the battle was fought until dusk. Norman sources mention that William had his army ready and armed through the night before the battle, expecting a surprise attack by the English.

The Norman organization of forces is better described, and it is known that William divided his army into groups by their origin. The left group was made of Bretons, who fought along with the troops from Anjou, Poitou, and Maine and were led by Alan the Red. The central group was constructed of Normans and led by Count William. He was surrounded by his cousins and other loyal nobility. The right group was under the command of William FitzOsbern and consisted of French soldiers who fought alongside troops from Flanders. The archers formed the front line, followed by infantry with long spears. Cavalry was held back as a reserve. The army was followed by clergymen and a plethora of servants who were not expected to fight. They were waiting at a safe distance, observing the battle.

The battle started with Norman archers shooting at the English shield wall. The archers didn't achieve much, considering that the English army was situated uphill on a slope. This meant that arrows would easily bounce off the shields. Since Harold's army did not have archers or had very few, Normans did not have arrows to pick up and reuse. William sent infantry to try and break the English shield wall, but they were met by thrown rocks, axes, and spears and were unable to approach. The cavalry was next, but they also failed to advance, and William was forced to order a retreat. A rumor started that the count was already dead, and Norman soldiers started panicking in their retreat while the English army pursued them. It is quite possible that the English soldiers' pursuit was spontaneous and that Harold did not order it. Hearing the rumor, William rode through his army, showing his face and yelling that he was still alive, boosting his army's morale and courage. Normans organized a counterattack against the English, who broke their ranks in pursuit. Harold's forces tried to reorganize on a hill but were quickly overwhelmed.

In the early afternoon, a break in the fighting occurred, and William seized the opportunity to change tactics. Inspired by the English army's methods, William tried sending cavalry first and pretending retreat to motivate the English army to break their ranks in another pursuit. After the Battle of Hastings, the feigned flight tactic was used regularly by Norman armies. The shield wall held, but this ploy did thin the line of housecarls. Further development of the battle is not certain, but some sources claim that three horses were killed under Duke William during the battle.

Harold, king of England, died during the battle, and historians presume it was near the end of the fighting. It is not quite clear exactly how the king died, but sources from 1080 mention an arrow to the eye. There is also a tapestry depicting the death of King Harold that contains two figures next to each other, one dying due to arrow in his eye, the other due to a sword. Which of the two figures represents the king is not known. It is also unknown who killed Harold, but it was probably a knight, possibly not even realizing who was in front of him during the battle frenzy. If in truth, he died due to an arrow, it would be impossible to say who shot it.

When their leader died, English forces started to collapse and could not keep the line. Noble houses and housecarls gathered around Harold's body and fought until the end, but many soldiers fled the battlefield. This was the end of the battle, even though Norman cavalry decided to pursue fleeing the English.

### The Aftermath of the Battle and Rebellions

After the battle, William expected that surviving English nobles would bow to him. Instead, Edgar Etheling (or Aetheling), last surviving heir to the house of Wessex, was proclaimed a king by the Witenagemot (Anglo-Saxon parliament), although he was never crowned. Angered, William started a march towards London in hopes he would capture it. At Southwark, he was attacked by an English force that was sent to stop his advance. He defeated this force but was unable to approach the London Bridge and was forced to go around. He crossed the Thames at Wallingford and accepted the submission of Stigand, Archbishop of Canterbury. London constantly sent forces out to attack William, but none of the attacks stopped his approach to the city's northwest side. As the Normans started closing in on London, Edgar Etheling's supporters started abandoning him and negotiating with William. In early December, the nobles gathered and decided to take the young Edgar to meet William and submit to him. Edgar did as he was asked and bowed to William at his coronation ceremony at Westminster Abbey in 1066. Edgar Etheling was given lands, and he remained in close vicinity to William the Conqueror but was never punished. The next year, William returned to Normandy with English prisoners, and Edgar was among them. However, the very next year, Edgar was back in England, where he may or may not have participated in rebellions that followed. He ended up in Scotland, where King Malcolm III Canmore married his sister Margaret. With this marriage, Edgar secured Scottish support in regaining the throne of England.

Upon William's departure for Normandy, he left control of England to his half-brother, Odo, and his supporter, William FitzOsbern. The English didn't wait long before they launched the first rebellion. It started in 1067 at Kent with an unsuccessful attack on Dover Castle. In Mercia, a landowner known as Eadric the Wild (or Silvaticus), together with the Welsh kings of Gwynedd and Powys, fought Norman forces in Hereford so ruthlessly that William decided to come back to England in 1068 and deal with the revolt personally. After subduing the rebels, William had Queen Matilda crowned at Westminster, which spoke to his consistently growing international stature. Later the same year, Edwin and Morcar, ex-earls of Mercia and Northumbria, raised a revolt on territories of Mercia. In Northumbria, a newly-appointed earl, Gospatric, also led an uprising in his own lands. William moved quickly against these rebellions and subdued them with the same tactics he used in the south of England, where he razed castles and garrisons.

In 1069, Edgar came back from Scotland and joined forces with Gospatric and Siward Barn, an English landowner. Together they massacred the new Earl of Northumbria, the Norman Robert de Comines, and his army. The Norman castellan of York was also killed, and rebels besieged the Castle of York. William hurried to bring help and managed to defeat the rebels outside of York, but he did not stop with the rebels. To prevent future uprisings, he entered the city and massacred its population. He oversaw the building of a new castle in York and reinforced the army in Northumbria before turning back south. Small rebellions occurred throughout the country for many more years, but William had no difficulties quelling them. It is interesting to note that rebels often took refuge in forests, sleeping under the open sky. This practice provides the basis for many legends of outlaws of the woods, Robin Hood, the most famous among them. The name of Eadric the Wild suggests he was one of the first rebels who inhabited the forests. Normans were the ones who called these rebel *silvatici* (the wild ones), and a legend grew that they preferred forests so that they do not grow soft in the comfort of houses and beds.

During 1070, William briefly settled in the region of Cheshire in Mercia, where he successfully quelled yet another rebellion and drove Edgar and his supporters back to Scotland. Upon returning to the south, he was visited by papal legates who re-crowned him, granting the pope's approval of his conquest of England. All his sins from the Battle of Hastings and other campaigns on English soil were forgiven by papal legates. Norman chronicles say William had papal approval of English conquest even before he crossed the English Channel in the first place, but there is no evidence to support this claim.

In 1069, a large Danish fleet sent by King Sweyn II landed in England, starting more rebellions across the country. The next year, Sweyn came to England in person to take control of his forces and join the rebels led by Hereward the Wake. However, Sweyn was easily discouraged from the attacks. William simply offered him a payment of Danegeld (a tribute to Viking raiders), after which the Danes returned home. The last resistance movement was organized in 1071 when Edgar and exiled rebels came back from Scotland and joined forces with Hereward the Wake. They were also joined by Morcar, whose brother Edwin was killed earlier. Hereward the Wake, the leader of the last rebellion, became a legend in English folklore. His base was on the Isle of Ely in East Anglia. He was ascribed a fantastical set of deeds, such as burning a tower with a witch to avoid a curse, masquerading as a potter to spy on the king,

and outwitting his nemesis, Frederick. All the stories that surround the persona of Hereward the Wake prove he was a leader who became a symbol of rebellion against Norman rule.

# Chapter 6 – The Consequences of the Norman Conquest

William conquered England, and, with the greed and appetite of a conqueror, he raised taxes and confiscated the estates of English nobles who were either killed for fighting against him in the Battle of Hastings or sent into exile. Many chose to flee to avoid punishment for fighting against William. Family members of deceased King Harold sought refuge in Ireland and used it as a base from which they tried to invade England unsuccessfully. The largest exodus of Anglo-Saxons happened in 1070 when 235 ships left for the Byzantine Empire, where they mostly served as mercenaries.

The confiscated lands served as rewards for the Normans who fought alongside William and were his most loyal supporters. The new taxes and overthrow of the English homeland were the cause of many rebellions throughout the country, but none of them were a serious threat to William's overrule. While some nobles and *thegns* decided to fight against William, others agreed to serve him. As a king of England, William was aware he needed domestic administrators who understood the temper of the English people. He kept the English sheriffs, and monasteries were still governed by local abbots. Regenbald, a royal official during the rule of Edward the Confessor, became William's chancellor. Although his name suggests he was either Norman or German, he was probably a naturalized foreigner in English court.

By 1086, only two English noble families were allowed to retain their lands, and this was achieved through collaboration with William's regime. They were Coleswain of Lincoln and Thurkill of Arden. All the other lands were given to Norman magnates, who in turn promised to supply the king with an army in times of need and with knights who would enter the king's service. English land was destined to produce support for the occupational army.

William implemented the law under which all the lands in England were owned by the king, and small landowners became land tenants. The taxes on land tenants were harsh, and many decided to abandon the fields and pastures they previously owned. The abandoned lands were soon inhabited by Norman families who decided to move to England and settle in these new lands of opportunity. The pattern of Norman colonization of England continued well into the 12th century. With the new settlers came a new language. Anglo-Norman, Old Norse heavily influenced by Old French, was introduced into English society. This was now the language of the ruling class of England. The most obvious change was in personal names. William, Robert, and Richard were now popular male names, while female names changed more slowly. When Scandinavians invaded England, the names of places changed rapidly, but this was not the case after the Norman invasion. For some reason, English cities, villages, and territories kept their names. Although many royal officials, artists, and merchants were bilingual and spoke both Norman and English, William himself never bothered to learn English, and the language was not well understood among the nobility. The Norman language became the language of the law, and as such, it used French words such as "crime," "contract," "master," "treason," and "felony." It was also the language of trade; words such as "money" and "payment" are also borrowed from French.

English laws continued to be valid, as Normans had no laws of their own. William declared the laws of Edward the Confessor still valid, and he also implemented some of the laws written in the time of King Cnut. In time, Normans introduced some of their own laws, but, mostly, they used the existing ones. Administration was another aspect of English rule that survived. Again in lack of their own system, the Normans were quick to accept the administrative structure that was already in place throughout England. The names changed, but the institutions stayed the same. *Thegns* were now called knights, but they continued to serve as masters and judges of the land. The shires, the hundred, and the tithing stayed the same. Taxes, though raised, worked exactly the same. Military service was also of English origin and did not change, although troops' training and housing were improved. Even the Witenagemot, the Anglo-Saxon parliament, remained unchanged and enjoyed its old privileges.

How life under the new regime changed for lower levels of society is largely unknown. Slavery was eliminated, and it completely disappeared by the 12$^{th}$ century. The most likely cause for the disappearance of slavery was the new taxes, which didn't allow nobles to maintain slaves in their households. Also, the church disapproved greatly of slavery, and the church had a tremendous influence on the nobility. The majority of free villagers suddenly fell under serfdom, a form of debt bondage. They could be sold and bought just like slaves, but they could maintain themselves. In return for their servitude, the lord of the estate they were serving would provide them with protection and enough land to provide for their own families. They were not allowed to sell that land; in fact, they had no right over their own lives and bodies. They were forbidden from leaving the land where they served and could marry only with the permission of their lord. The villages became more centered and entirely replaced scattered farms. Towns were growing in size and numbers as they attracted new settlers. The status of peasant women of the 11$^{th}$ century is completely unknown, but it probably didn't change much with the Norman invasion. Noble ladies, on the other hand, had the right to own land and to influence politics through their kinships and relationships. Some were even allowed to dispose of their property as they wished, without the permission of male relatives.

In the first years after the Norman invasion, the overall appearance of English and Norman people differed, and not just in clothing and armor. English men wore their hair long, while Normans wore it short, even shaven. The English managed to influence Normans, and soon, through the intermingling of people, it became impossible to notice the difference.

The landscape of England also changed. The Normans built castles in their own style—square buildings with extremely thick walls and small windows. The castle was used as living quarters for the aristocracy, a courthouse, a fortress, a barracks for soldiers, and a prison for law offenders. The castles were built everywhere throughout the country as an effort to fortify hot spots where rebellions occurred. Castles continued to serve the same purpose throughout the ages, and the *Anglo-Saxon Chronicle* mentions that William created such safety in England that one could cross the whole kingdom and not fear for one's gold or one's life.

Normans invented the "forest law," which stated that all animals and fruits in the kingdom belonged to the king. No one was permitted to hunt or pick fruits, not even to gather firewood. If caught, perpetrators would be blinded. At the beginning of Norman rule, this law included only forests. However, the aristocracy soon built rabbit and deer parks, and almost one-third of the country fell under this law. For example, the entirety of Essex was enclosed and served as the monarch's preserve.

The church was an essential part of William's kingdom. Numerous Norman reforms were introduced through the institute of religion. Many new churches and monasteries were built, and Norman clergy were the ones who inhabited them. By 1086, only three out of twenty-one abbots were English. Norman priests and abbots did not look at their English colleagues with sympathy. Some even refused to celebrate English saints, calling them old-fashioned. While numerous Norman abbots were cruel to the English monks, some were quite the opposite. The abbot of Selby, for example, helped in building the church for his community. He dressed as a simple worker and shared meals with his commune. At the end of the week, he gave away his pay to the poor. An Italian, Lanfranc, was posted as Archbishop of Canterbury. He gained the new king's trust since he was the one who embarked on the journey to ask the pope for approval of William and Matilda's marriage. The couple seems to have been closely related, which the church did not approve of. He drew up the first draft of the canon law, which pleased William, who then ordered that all matters of the church should be addressed in ecclesiastical courts. Lanfranc was also the one who helped William keep the English church independent of the pope in Rome. However, when it came to internal matters of state, he remained neutral. His goal in life was to eradicate corruption from the church and enforce celibacy on the clergy. He prohibited marriage for the English clergy in 1076.

By order of King William the Conqueror in 1086, a survey of the whole kingdom was taken and recorded. This included much of England and some parts of Wales. The book was named "Great Survey," but it is remembered by its popular name, "Domesday Book." The survey was written in Medieval Latin, but some of the terms from certain dialects had no Latin translation and were written in their original form. The purpose of this survey was to determine the exact taxes owed to the crown since the time of King Edward's reign and to have a clear record of the distributed lands after its redistribution to the Normans. The book held the record of all livestock and lands owned by everyone in the kingdom, and it was used for raising taxes as well as the more accurate placement of military forces.

William died in the autumn of 1087 while on a campaign in Normandy, but he did not die in battle. He either fell ill with a fever or got injured by the pommel of his saddle, which may have burst some internal organ. At the first signs of illness, William was taken to the monastery of Saint Gervase in Rouen, where he suffered for three weeks before dying on September 9, 1087.

William named his eldest son Robert the heir of the Duchy of Normandy. England he left to his third son, William Rufus. His fourth son got a consolation prize in money. With his father's letter to Lanfranc, young William set out for England on September 7 or 8. Before his death, William ordered that all his prisoners be freed. Upon death, the body of William was moved to the Abbey of Saint-Etienne, also known as the Abbaye aux Hommes, where he wished to be buried. The funeral was attended only by clergy and his youngest son Henry, as other dignitaries had run home to deal with their own affairs. There were two incidents during William's funeral. First, a citizen showed up at the doors of the abbey, claiming that his lands were illegally granted to the church by William. This man was proven right and was compensated. The second happened when William's body was lowered into the tomb. It was so big that it couldn't fit. While the clergy were pushing his body into the tomb, it burst and released a foul stench that made everyone run out of the cathedral.

# Chapter 7 – Race for Power

William II Rufus

Portrayal of William II

https://en.wikipedia.org/wiki/William_II_of_England#/media/File:William_II_of _England.jpg

The death of William the Conqueror was followed by disorder. The most immediate consequence was the war between his sons over control of both England and Normandy. The Ducal authority was lost in Normandy, and nobility managed to seize much of the power.

William the Conqueror had decided to divide the lands he ruled among his two sons. William II, also known as William Rufus, became king of England, while his brother Robert was given charge of Normandy. This divide presented much trouble for nobles who owned lands in both kingdoms, especially because William and Robert showed signs of rivalry from a young age. Nobles had to work hard to please both lords, but the task was impossible. They were always in fear of displeasing one or the other ruler. The solution to the troubles of the aristocracy was to once again unite England and Normandy, under a single ruler. Only a year after ascending the throne of England, William Rufus was facing a rebellion. In 1088, Bishop Odo of Bayeux, half-brother of William the Conqueror, led an uprising that aimed to replace William Rufus with his brother Robert. But William II had the support of all the bishops of England and some of the major Norman magnates in England.

The rebels had their own castles in the territory of England, which they reinforced. Their plan was to raid neighboring territories to challenge King William to respond with the army. In case the king did not respond, the plan was to continue attacking English lands and cause feudal anarchy, which the king would have to address sooner or later. But the king managed to divide his enemies. He promised that those who sided with him would be given money and land. Greedy Normans could not decline such an offer. William also appealed to the English people, promising the best laws possible that would work to their advantage, if only they supplied his army. With the divided enemy and secured support from the people, William finally attacked the rebels. The siege of their power center, Pevensey Castle in Sussex, lasted for six weeks. William was victorious, and he even captured Odo, the rebel leader. The next for the taking was Rochester Castle in Kent, and yet again, William did not encounter serious opposition. Luck played a part in his easy victory over the rebels: forces that Robert sent from Normandy to help Odo never arrived due to bad weather.

After the rebellion, William showed mercy to the nobles who were fighting against him. Odo was exiled to Normandy and was never to set foot on English soil for as long as he lived. In this manner, William exiled nobles who were not useful to him and showed mercy to those who had the potential of being great allies. Some were even allowed to keep their lands and estates in England, while those who joined the king's side during the rebellion were rewarded with land and money. William used the English army to crush the rebellion, and English people provided supplies for the army. With this act, he managed to rekindle the English national identity and gain their trust. The English people were not just fighting for their lands anymore; they were fighting for their king.

In 1091, William II decided to invade Normandy and challenge his brother's rule. He managed to take part of the lands, but he also made peace with his brother. He promised Robert he would help him take back Maine, but soon enough, he abandoned these plans. Until the end of his life, William was determined to defend his interests in Normandy, and he was often involved in the politics of France. In 1097, Robert decided to join the Crusades, and he left Normandy to William as a regency. To support his brother's decision, William raised additional taxes on the people of England, who resented him for it. William served as regent of Normandy until his death in 1100.

In 1091, and again in 1093, William faced an invasion from Scotland. Malcolm III of Scotland hoped he could claim a large part of northern English territory but was repulsed by William's army. During the invasion of 1093, both Malcolm and his son Edward were killed, and the throne of Scotland was seized by his brother Donald. However, William gave his support to Malcolm's second son, Duncan II, who managed to hold power for a short period of time. He was succeeded by Malcolm's fourth son, Edgar, who also had the support of William II. With the help of the English army, Edgar managed to remove Donald in 1097. To show gratefulness to William, he recognized his authority and regularly attended the English court.

William died during a hunt on August 2, 1100, in the New Forest. He was killed by an arrow that pierced his lungs, but whether it was an accident or a deliberate shot remains unproven. Later chronicles attribute the shot to a noble, Walter Tirel, who took a wild shot at the stag but, instead, hit the king. The accuracy of this report is questionable, as the chroniclers who wrote it lived at much later times. Accidents were nothing unusual during a hunt, and it is quite possible that this is how William Rufus died. Historians also credit William's younger brother Henry for the murder of the king, as he is the one who would inherit the throne of England. Although the theory of plot and murder is an interesting one, there is not enough evidence to support it. The official account of William's death remains a hunting accident.

During his life, William never took a wife or even a mistress. He never fathered a child, and he had no heir apparent. This fact is what later started the rumor that he was a homosexual, but he was never accused of it during his reign. Future chroniclers go as far as to call him a sodomite, but this might be the biased opinion of clergy since William was in constant dispute with the church. However, the lack of women in William's life might have also been a sign that he had taken a vow of chastity and celibacy, which was not uncommon for people of the Middle Ages. Still, historians admit it was certainly uncommon for a king. He was expected to get

married at least for political purposes, and it is possible that the king was just waiting for the right opportunity for the marriage.

## Henry I of England

Portrayal of Henry I

https://upload.wikimedia.org/wikipedia/commons/c/ca/Henry_I_Cotton_Claudius_D._ii%2C_f._45v..jpg

When William II Rufus died, his younger brother Henry rushed to Winchester, where he persuaded the English barons to support his claim to the throne instead of his brother Robert, who was on his way back from the Crusades. He claimed that even though he was the younger of the two brothers, he was the rightful heir under the right of porphyrogeniture. This meant that since he was born after William the Conqueror became king, he was the rightful heir. His brother Robert had been born before their father conquered England. When he convinced the aristocracy to support him, he seized the royal treasury.

Henry was crowned in haste on August 5, 1100. He was thirty-one years old when he started his rule. A few months later, he was married to Matilda, the daughter of Malcolm III of Scotland. The marriage was politically suitable, but chroniclers also mention that the couple had an emotional relationship, too. Maybe this was the reason Henry trusted her enough to make her regent of England while he was away. She proved to be an efficient queen, not just in title but in action. She often addressed the councils and even presided over a number of them while acting as a regent. She was also an enthusiastic supporter of the arts. Even though Henry had two children with his queen, he often indulged in the pleasures of mistresses, and he had many. With his mistresses, he had approximately nine sons and thirteen daughters, some of whom he recognized as his own and supported through their lives.

By July 1101, Robert formed a fleet and was ready to cross the English Channel to attack his brother Henry. The support of the aristocracy to the new English king was partial and unreliable. During the next few months, Henry made them all swear allegiance to him once again. The anticipated landing site of Robert's forces was at Pevensey, and that is where Henry mobilized his army. Because the English army wasn't used to cavalry, Henry took it upon himself to train them on how to oppose cavalry charges. Many of the barons were still contemplating who to support in the upcoming fight and didn't come to the military assembly. Anselm, Archbishop of Canterbury, had to remind them of the religious importance of their allegiance to the king. But Robert's fleet landed at Portsmouth and surprised Henry. He had only a few hundred men with him but was soon joined by the armies of English barons who chose to support him.

The armies of England and Normandy met at Alton, Hampshire, and instead of fighting, they started peace negotiations. Robert and Henry made an agreement known as the Treaty of Alton, in which Robert recognized Henry as the king of England. Henry had to renounce his territories in Normandy, except Domfront. He also agreed to pay Robert a yearly salary until the end of his life. Although there was no army confrontation, Henry was angered by the disloyalty his barons had shown. To punish them, he seized their lands, and some of them were exiled to Normandy.

During the next few years, Normandy fell into chaos and started disintegrating. Henry was inspired to start a confrontation with his brother once again, and, to provoke him, he sent his friend Robert Fitzhamon to disturb the politics. Fitzhamon was caught and imprisoned, which gave Henry an excuse to invade Normandy. He managed to persuade King Philip of France to stay neutral while he gathered the support of Normandy's neighboring counts. Henry proceeded by occupying western Normandy and advancing toward Bayeux. Robert agreed to negotiations, but they were fruitless. The fight continued until Christmas when Henry decided to go back to England. In 1106, he was back and launched another invasion of Normandy. Another attempt at negotiations failed, and the Battle of Tinchebray took place. The battle had been raging for only one hour when Duke Robert was taken prisoner. But Henry had no legal power to depose his brother as Duke of Normandy. Instead, he excused his actions by claiming he only came to help troubled Normandy and had acted like a king of England. He proclaimed himself the guardian of Normandy and never used the title duke.

In November of 1120, Henry's only son and heir died when his ship sank just outside the Norman harbor. He did not want one of his various nephews to inherit the throne of England. Instead, he announced he would marry again, with Adeliza of Louvain, in hopes she would give him another son. They were married in Windsor Castle in 1121 but never had any children. His daughter from a previous wife was married to the emperor of the Holy Roman Empire, Henry, who died in 1125. Matilda was recalled to England, where her father named her his heir. However, Matilda faced strong opposition, as it was very unusual for a woman to inherit her father's throne. Henry was joyous when Matilda gave birth to two sons–two possible heirs to the throne of England.

Henry I of England died while on a hunt in Normandy in December of 1135. The chronicles mention that he fell ill due to overeating on lampreys, despite his physician's advice. Henry's entrails were buried at the property of Notre-Dame-du-Pré, while his body was taken to England and entombed at Reading Abbey.

**Anarchy in England**

A succession crisis followed the death of Henry I. His nephew, Stephen of Blois, rushed to seize power in England before Empress Matilda could leave Normandy. Stephen was the son of Adela of Normandy, daughter of William the Conqueror, and his father was a count in northern France. Stephen was the fourth son of this couple, and as such, did not own any lands or titles. Therefore, he joined the court of Henry I and served the king in his campaigns. In return for his service, the king granted Stephen some lands, and he married Matilda of Boulogne, heiress to the Count of Boulogne. Stephen had one younger brother, who became the Bishop of Winchester and supported his brother's claim to the throne.

The people of London claimed the right to elect the king of England, and they elected Stephen. With the support of the church, Stephen was able even to justify his breaking of the oath to the dead king, that he would support Empress Matilda. His brother, Henry, argued that the oath was needed in that time to ensure the stability of the kingdom. As the kingdom no longer had stability, the oath wasn't valid. Henry even went so far as to claim that the late king changed his mind on his deathbed and proclaimed Stephen his successor. Hugh Bigod, Earl of Norfolk, supported this claim, which was obvious deceit. Stephen was crowned on December 26, 1135, and was confirmed by Pope Innocent II the next year.

In Normandy, the nobility gathered and discussed supporting Theobald, grandson of William the Conqueror, as the true heir to the English Kingdom as well as the Duchy of Normandy. They argued that Theobald was more suitable to the throne than Matilda because she was a woman. But the very next day, the news of

Stephen's coronation reached Normandy, and all the barons withdrew their support from Theobald, as they did not wish to divide England from Normandy by opposing to the new king. The barons of Normandy still had estates in both countries, and they needed peace to prosper.

Upon his coronation, Stephen had to deal with those who would oppose him immediately. In the north of England, Matilda's uncle, David I of Scotland, invaded and took some key strongholds. After a brief fight, an agreement was made in which David would return all conquered lands except Carlisle. In return, Stephen confirmed possessions in England that David's son had claimed. Still, early during his reign, Stephen had to put down numerous uprisings–the major ones in southwestern England. Because of the unrest in his kingdom, Stephen never got the chance to go to Normandy and claim the duchy, although he did send a representative in his name. In 1136, Normandy was attacked by Geoffrey, Count of Anjou, who raided and burned the lands instead of claiming them. Stephen finally traveled to Normandy in 1137, where he met with King Louis VI. They formed an alliance to fight the growing power of the Angevins, or House of Anjou. This was also an opportunity for Stephen to ask the king of France to recognize his son as Duke of Normandy, which he gladly did.

In 1138, the first fighting between the forces of Stephen and Matilda broke out. Robert of Gloucester, the illegitimate son of Henry I, who remained Matilda's supporter, started an uprising against the king. Interestingly, he managed to start a rebellion from afar, while staying in Normandy. This uprising would lead the whole kingdom into a civil war. At the same time, David of Scotland invaded northern England once more, declaring his support to his niece Matilda. In Normandy, Geoffrey of Anjou invaded again. Stephen was quick to respond to these uprisings, but he decided to concentrate on England and retake the territories Robert's rebels had claimed. To avoid separating his army, he decided to negotiate with David and grant him and his son both Northumbria and Cumbria in exchange for peace along the Scottish border.

In 1139, Geoffrey and Matilda secured their power over Normandy and started preparations for an invasion of England. Finally, in August, the army crossed the English Channel and landed at Arundel in West Sussex on the invitation of Dowager Queen Adeliza. Matilda stayed in Arundel Castle, while her half-brother, Robert, marched northwest to gather rebels and supporters and form an army. But Stephen responded immediately and besieged the castle in which Matilda was staying. The king's brother, Bishop Henry, persuaded both sides to agree to a truce. The details of this truce are unknown, but Empress Matilda was released from the siege and, together with her household, was allowed to go northwest and reunite with Robert. It is not known why Stephen decided to simply release his opponent, but historians argue that he saw true danger in Robert, not Matilda.

However, Matilda had gained a block of territories from Gloucester and Bristol to Devon and Cornwall. London was threatened to be next for the taking by Matilda and Robert, and Stephen had to react. He tried to take over some key castles and block the approach to the Thames River but was under constant attacks by Matilda's supporters. In the end, he had to give up his campaign and return to his capital to stabilize the situation. The fighting continued for years until, finally, a peace attempt was made. The clergy urged Stephen to accept any conditions, but he remained stubborn, claiming that peace was unacceptable, and no treaty was signed.

In early 1141, Stephen besieged the Lincoln Castle, and Robert of Gloucester came to the king's position with a large force. The Battle of Lincoln followed on February 2$^{nd}$ of the same year. Stephen dismounted his cavalry to form an infantry wall and even fought on foot, side by side with his soldiers. The king had initial success in the battle, but Robert prevailed. He used cavalry to surround the center of Stephen's army, and the king was trapped. At this point of the battle, many barons who supported the king fled, but Stephen continued to fight. The battle ended when, after a long fight, Stephen was taken as a prisoner. Empress Matilda started preparing for her coronation as queen of England. She gained the support of Stephen's brother, Bishop Henry, whom she promised full control of church business. Henry gave Matilda the royal treasury and even excommunicated those of Stephen's supporters who refused to switch sides.

Matilda was to be crowned in London in June, but when she approached the city, the people rose against her. She was forced to flee to Oxford, together with her supporters. Stephen's supporters gathered around his wife, Queen Matilda, and together they entered London after the city expelled the empress. Bishop Henry once again switched sides and offered his support to Stephen's wife. The queen was very successful in gathering loyalists, and she even managed to negotiate her husband's release. Together, Stephen and his queen besieged Oxford Castle, where Empress Matilda was staying. Right before Christmas in 1142, Empress Matilda managed to sneak out of the castle and cross the frozen river on foot, escaping to the safety of Wallingford. Her garrison at Oxford surrendered to Stephen the next day.

The civil war in England reached a stalemate that lasted from 1143 until 1146. The fighting kept on, and at the Battle of Wilton, Stephen almost got captured once more. He again lost to the superiority of Robert's cavalry. In the meantime, in Normandy, Geoffrey of Anjou secured his power and was even recognized as duke by French King Louis VII.

Robert of Gloucester died peacefully in 1147, and Matilda returned to Normandy. The civil war was officially over, but smaller campaigns still occurred. Without Robert and Matilda, their supporters in England felt little need to fight. Most of the battles were small, local uprisings that were easily quelled. Barons who supported Matilda were left on their own and started individual negotiations with Stephen, with many successfully concluded. Matilda stayed in Normandy and focused on promoting her son as heir to the throne of England while, in England, Stephen was resolving the issue of his family and succession. Stephen preferred the French tradition of crowning the son before the king dies, but he was strongly opposed by the clergy. Even the pope banned any changes in the English tradition of succession, and Archbishop Theobald refused to crown Stephen's eldest son Eustace without the pope's agreement. For his refusal, the archbishop was imprisoned and then exiled in Flanders.

Matilda's son, Henry FitzEmpress, returned to England in 1153 and besieged Stephen's castle at Malmesbury with the small army. Henry secured the control of the southwest of England, the Midlands, and some territories in the north. In July of the same year, Stephen gathered a large force and confronted Henry at Wallingford Castle. However, the battle was postponed when clergy intervened and sued for peace. Stephen and Henry agreed to talk privately about a possible end to the war, but the king's son, Eustace, was furious with the outcome. He abandoned his father and started preparing an army for his own campaign. However, after only one month, he fell ill and died. His death was convenient to the peace seekers, as his claim to the throne was removed. Stephen now recognized Henry FitzEmpress as his heir, adopting him as his son. His younger son, William, had to renounce his claim on the throne and pay homage to Henry.

Stephen fell ill and died on October 25, 1154. Henry was in Normandy at the time and did not feel the need to hurry back to England. He postponed his travels until December. Upon his arrival, he was quickly crowned as king of England, together with his wife, Eleanor. The barons swore fealty to the new king during the gathering of the royal court in April of 1155. Henry II was the legitimate heir of Stephen, and upon taking the crown, he started rebuilding the war-torn kingdom. England had been devastated by civil war, and occasional raiding in the north still happened. The economy of the kingdom was falling apart, as all pretenders to the throne had issued their own coins during the war. The royal treasury was almost empty when Henry II inherited it. The king's income had declined during the war, and the money had been spent mostly on supplying the army, leaving little for Henry II to use in his rebuilding of the kingdom.

# Chapter 8 – Henry II

Henry was the eldest child of Empress Matilda and her second husband, Geoffrey Plantagenet, Count of Anjou. He was born in 1133, the grandson of English King Henry I. He was also the adopted son and heir to Stephen, the king of England who seized the throne upon the death of Henry I. Henry II was crowned on December 19, 1154, a few months after Stephen's death.

During the reign of King Stephen, England was torn by civil war. The leaders of Wales and Scotland took advantage of this unrest to invade and conquer lands in England. The first task Henry II undertook was to regain these lands. In 1157, Malcolm IV of Scotland, pressured by the new English king, had to return the lands he had conquered in the north. Henry was quick to reinforce the border with Scotland by erecting new fortifications. It was a more difficult task to restore Anglo-Norman supremacy in Wales, where Henry II had to fight two battles, in 1157 and 1158. Finally, Welsh princes gave up on their conquered lands in England and acknowledged Henry's supremacy.

In 1158, Henry II returned to Normandy, where he had spent much of his childhood and youth. His task was to secure his lands in Normandy and deal with any possible uprisings. While there, he agreed to betroth his eldest surviving son, Henry the Young King (or Young Henry), to Margaret, the daughter of French King Louis VII. Henry II's power grew in France, and he seized the opportunity to establish his dominance in the Duchy of Brittany.

He planned to take over Toulouse but had no power to directly attack King Louis VII, who also showed interest in this region. Instead, a peace treaty was achieved, and it was overseen by Pope Alexander III in 1162. Henry was satisfied with confirming his son's betrothal to a French princess, which gave him access to Vexin territory in France.

Following the development of the events in France, Henry II ruled lands historians today call the Angevin Empire. It includes the French territories of Normandy, Brittany, and some smaller land possessions, as well as all England and parts of Wales, Scotland, and Ireland. Henry ruled many of these territories by proxy, and what his empire lacked was centralized power. Henry relied on family connections and the loyalty of his barons. Each territory was ruled by its local customs, but Henry often visited. What followed were governmental reforms or local administrative changes. Each territory was ruled by a local seneschal or a justiciar, who was often one of Henry's family members. Under them were local officials who dealt with the day-to-day tasks of government. All these officials were connected to Henry by a network of messengers, and everyone was permitted to petition the king directly.

When it came to making major decisions, Henry II would employ his royal court to act as a great council. The task of the great council was to advise the king, but it is not clear how much freedom the council had to act beyond advising. At the beginning of his reign, Henry decided to keep all the administrators of King Stephen's reign and some of those from his grandfather Henry I's reign. Soon enough, he would replace them all, bringing new people into the positions of power. Usually, these would be illegitimate members of his family or close and loyal friends. In Normandy, he relied on bishops and other clergy to run the official tasks of the duchy. Henry was a ruthless ruler, and he was quick to punish people who disobeyed him, especially clergy and barons.

However, he also granted his patronage to the lands that pleased him, and these territories would prosper greatly.

The law changed significantly during the reign of Henry II. He reformed the legal system of the Kingdom of England, by which royal justice was greatly expanded. For Henry, the delivery of justice was one of the primary roles of the king, and he was said to enjoy the law. At the end of his reign, Ranulf de Glanvill wrote a treatise on English Law, remembered simply as the treatise of Glanvill. After the civil war, Henry resolved many of the land disputes himself. He did rely on existing laws and tradition, but many of these cases demanded his personal involvement because they were misjudged.

When it came to the economy of the Kingdom of England, Henry II heavily taxed the populace for the first eleven years of his rule. The taxes were necessary to fill the royal treasury, which was emptied during the civil war. To hire mercenaries and finance the building of new castles and fortifications, Henry borrowed money, mostly from moneylenders in Rouen. He restored the system of financing royalty that his grandfather Henry I had used. To stimulate trade, he issued the new Awbridge silver penny as his currency. In 1180, the short-cross penny was issued. Henry gave direct control of the mints to royal officials, who passed the profits directly to the royal treasury. Issuing new coins had the long-term effect of stimulating both trade and inflation in England.

## Thomas Becket

King Henry II and Thomas Becket

https://upload.wikimedia.org/wikipedia/commons/4/45/BecketHenryII.jpg

Theobald of Bec, Archbishop of Canterbury, died in 1161, and Henry II put his chancellor, Thomas Becket, in that position. Henry was hoping that Becket would restore royal supremacy over the church, as the two were in very good relations. However, Thomas Becket changed his whole lifestyle when he became the new archbishop. He even resigned his chancellorship. Formerly an ostentatious figure, he changed into a humble man who lived as an ascetic. Becket didn't just change his lifestyle; he also immediately stopped supporting Henry when it came to his royal rights over the church. Instead, Becket came to champion the church's independence.

The main point of dispute between Becket and the king was what to do with the clergy who committed secular crimes. One-fifth of the male population was considered clergy by the church, even though the majority only took "minor orders." Becket argued that all men who were considered clergy, even if they took only a minor order, shouldn't be dealt with by secular powers. Only the church could judge them for crimes, whether secular or ecclesiastical.

Henry believed this practice would deprive him of the ability to govern his kingdom effectively, and he strongly opposed Becket's idea. The king had support from the previous Archbishop of Canterbury on this matter. Theobald of Bec even declared to the papacy in 1154 that the English custom was to have secular courts try clerics.

There were many other points of dispute between Becket and the king, and the two kept clashing whenever the opportunity arose. Becket took action to recover the lands that once belonged to the church. He had no regard for the rights of current landowners, which caused many petitions to the king and added to the already-existing tension between the two. Another example is when Becket excommunicated a royal tenant-in-chief who claimed the right to appoint the clerics in the churches on his lands. The king issued a statement that no tenant-in-chief could be excommunicated without royal approval. Becket fought this statement but, in the end, was forced to submit to it.

In 1163, Henry II allowed Becket to voice his concerns about the governance of the English church. He summoned the church representatives, who stood by Becket and disagreed with the king. The king asked them to observe traditional English customs, but the clergy said they would not, since the customs conflicted with canon law. Angry, Henry took his son, Henry the Young King, from Becket's custody. He also confiscated all royal honors Becket had once held, thus effectively dismissing him from royal favor. Both King Henry II and Becket spent the next year securing allies. The king managed to sway some bishops to take his side, while Becket prepared ties to the lands on the continent, where he could seek refuge if the need arose. Pope Alexander III refused to meddle in the dispute between the king and the church, leaving them to resolve their differences with each other. To achieve a compromise, Henry wanted to employ clergy to write down English law customs, which would be presented to the church council. Becket agreed and even accepted the customs. Following his example, bishops swore to follow the customs that became known as Constitutions of Clarendon. This constitution forbade the clergy to travel without royal permission, which is what Thomas Becket tried to do in 1164. He was preparing for a journey to France when he was arrested. Additional charges were raised by a nobleman whose lands Becket had confiscated earlier. Under the pressure of other bishops, Becket accepted sentencing for all the land disputes in which he was involved. Even more charges were brought against Becket: he was charged with financial mismanagement during the time he was a chancellor, as well as with not following the Constitutions. He was found guilty on both charges. Thomas Becket refused these sentences and decided to go into exile.

Becket reached Sens in France, where each side had the opportunity to present its case to Pope Alexander III. Becket was not ordered to go back to England, but Henry II wasn't ordered to back down. The pope was still trying to be neutral regarding their dispute. Becket chose Pontigny in France as his place of exile, and Henry ordered the exile for Becket's whole family and household. The bishops who followed Becket lost their properties in England, as the king confiscated them.

While in exile, Becket continued pursuing a resolution for his dispute with the king, but the king was in no rush to reach peace with Becket. In 1166, Becket threatened divine punishment for the king if he didn't show enthusiasm for solving the problem. He even went so far as to excommunicate some of Henry's advisors and clerical servants, even bishops who had granted their support to the king. Henry was forced to write letters to Pope Alexander III, asking him to absolve the excommunications. The pope sent papal legates, who were charged with listening to both sides and reaching a peaceful conclusion. It took four years for the legates to negotiate a resolution. In the end, the pope granted his favor to King Henry II, as he needed English support in the dispute he had with the

German emperor. In 1167, the papal legates met with Becket, who refused to accept their judgment. The negotiations were halted, and the king, with his bishops, was forced to appeal to the pope once again. In 1169 Becket continued excommunicating English bishops and royal officials, even though the pope asked him to do no hostile acts that will endanger further negotiations. In August of that year, serious negotiations started between Henry and Becket, but to no avail.

On June 14, 1170, Henry the Young King was crowned the "Young King" of England while his father was still alive. Breaking the tradition of having the Archbishop of Canterbury perform the coronation, Henry employed the Archbishop of York. After coronation took place, Pope Alexander III granted approval to Becket to lay an interdict on all England as punishment. The interdict meant that all England was prohibited from performing the rites and services of the church. To avoid such punishment, Henry II agreed to resume negotiations with Becket. The archbishop was permitted to come back to England. However, before landing on English soil, Becket excommunicated Archbishop Roger of York and bishops Josceline of Salisbury and Foliot of London. The new excommunications angered Henry, who asked if anyone would rid him of the priest, meaning Becket. Four knights of Henry's court in Normandy arranged their journey to Canterbury, England, where they murdered Becket.

With Becket dealt with, Henry negotiated the dispute over church questions directly with Pope Alexander III, who asked the king to join the crusade. Henry also agreed to dispose of all customs from English law that did not suit the church. The king had to perform penance publicly on July 12, 1174. He confessed his sins at Canterbury, and then all present bishops had to hit him with a rod five times. Each of the eighty monks of Canterbury had to give the king three blows with the rod.

## The Great Revolt and succession problems

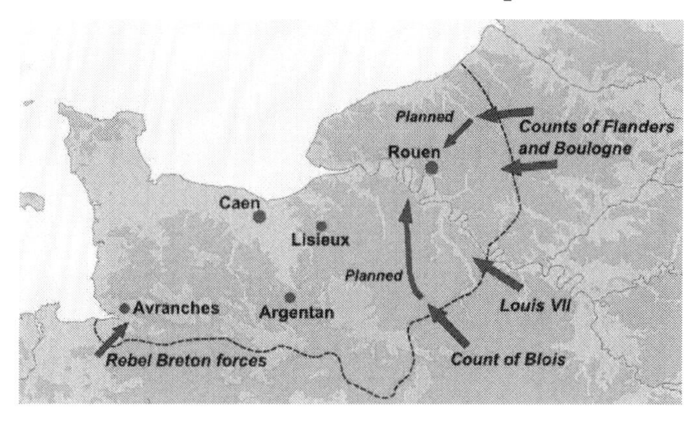


Events in Normandy 1173

https://en.wikipedia.org/wiki/Henry_II_of_England#/media/File:Great_Revolt_Normandy_1173.png

By 1173, Henry II of England had four surviving legitimate sons: Henry the Young King, Richard, who would become known as "The Lionheart," Geoffrey, and John "Lackland." Even though Young Henry was already crowned Young King of England, he had no resources of his own. He had many knights protecting him, but no means to reward them for their service. Because of this, he was anxious to rule on his own as a rightful king of England. When his father decided to take three castles that were meant for Young Henry and give them to his youngest brother, John, in preparations for his marriage, Young Henry rebelled. He was encouraged by various nobles and royal officials, who saw the opportunity for personal gain in a power shift from father to son. His mother, Queen Eleanor, who disputed her husband's decision, joined the cause and openly supported Young Henry. In March 1173, Henry the Young King and his brothers Richard and Geoffrey joined the court of French King Louis VII. In France, the brothers created an alliance with various counts, promising lands in England. The plan was to seize the kingdom by breaking it apart.

The first fighting started in April of 1173 when the armies of the counts of Flanders and Boulogne invaded Normandy from the east.

Louis VII and his son-in-law, the Young King Henry, attacked from the south, while the Bretons were charged with taking the west. Although well-planned, each of the attacks was repelled by the army of Normandy. The Count of Boulogne died in the battle. Negotiations between Henry II and his son Young Henry followed but achieved nothing.

The Earl of Leicester took charge of the rebels in Normandy. He hired Flemish mercenaries and crossed the English Channel to join the barons who rebelled in England. However, he never met his allies. Instead, his army was attacked by the English forces that were on their way south from Scotland. The Earl of Leicester was defeated, and his forces were destroyed.

The fighting continued in 1174 when the Earl of Huntington became the leader of the rebellion and tried to conquer northern England. Henry II was fighting his enemies in Normandy but had to turn back to England when Nottingham and Norwich were torched. After completing public penance for the death of Thomas Becket, Henry II took upon himself the task of breaking the rebellion. He gathered a large army and marched to each stronghold held by rebels to obtain their surrenders. The revolt lasted for eighteen months, and the records say around twenty castles across England were demolished. The blame was put not on the Young Henry, but on the barons who advised the inexperienced young king for their own gain. Henry II went back to Normandy, where he negotiated with his sons, and all three of them recognized him as their lord and returned to his service.

After the Great Revolt, Henry recognized his son Richard as Duke of Aquitaine in 1179. His other son, Geoffrey, married Constance of Brittany and became the Duke of Brittany in 1181. Through the Great Revolt and later, John followed his father and was observed as Henry's favorite child. The king bestowed more and more lands upon John, and in 1177, he made him the Lord of Ireland. Young King Henry spent this time traveling Europe and enjoying tournaments and other competitions, playing no role in governing England. He was greatly unsatisfied with his lack of power. In 1182, Young Henry asked to be granted lands, which would help him support himself and his household, but King Henry II refused. Instead, he promised to increase his son's allowance. This was not enough for Young Henry, who now demanded his brother Richard pay him homage. Richard refused, as he didn't see how Henry had any claim over Aquitaine but was forced by his father to comply. Angered, Young Henry refused to accept his brother's homage. Instead, he formed an alliance with the barons of Aquitaine who were unsatisfied with Richard's rule. Geoffrey joined Young Henry in the cause and paid for a mercenary army from Brittany. By 1183, open war broke out, and King Henry II and Richard had to defend Aquitaine. However, before any significant moves were made, Young King Henry fell suddenly ill and died, ending the conflict.

King Henry II had to make new arrangements for the succession, and he named his son Richard as heir. However, he did not rush to name him junior king, as with Young Henry. Instead, Richard had no power until his father's death. John, Henry's favorite child, became the Duke of Aquitaine, while Geoffrey remained in control of Brittany since he had gained it by marriage. Until the end of his days, Henry II was in constant conflict with his son Richard. He even considered renouncing Richard as his heir and giving the title to his youngest son John. However, Richard sided with the French King Philip Augustus, who had no love for Henry and supported Richard's claim to the throne. Together, they planned to attack Henry in Normandy, but the English king fell ill with a bleeding ulcer, which would prove to be fatal. The dying king wished to die in peace in Anjou rather than having to deal with war in Normandy. He met with Philip and Richard at Ballan and offered his complete surrender. He recognized Richard as his heir and paid homage to Philip. Upon hearing that Richard had the support of his brother John all along, Henry gave in to the fever and died on July 6, 1189.

Henry II of England was a hated king, and there was little grief upon his death. He bullied his court officials and often displayed bursts of temper. For this, he was criticized by his opposition—and even by some officials within his own court. When his successor Richard left to join the Third Crusade, the Angevin Empire fell apart under the rule of his favorite child, John.

# Chapter 9 – Richard and John

Richard's Coronation in Westminster Abbey

https://en.wikipedia.org/wiki/Richard_I_of_England#/media/File:Richard_L%C3%B6wenhez,_Salbung_zum_K%C3%B6nig.jpg

Upon the death of Henry II, his son Richard was appointed Duke of Normandy on July 20, 1189, and then crowned king of England on September 3rd of the same year. The coronation took place at Westminster Abbey. Tradition did not allow Jews to attend the ceremony, but some Jewish leaders tried to present gifts to the new king. They were kicked out of the court, but not before they were beaten. A rumor started that Richard ordered that all the Jews be killed, and the people of London started attacking Jewish houses. Many Jews were killed, their houses were burned, and some were forcefully converted to Christianity. Upon hearing of the unrest, Richard punished everyone who was caught acting against the Jews. The converted individuals were permitted to return to Judaism. Richard planned to join the crusade but was afraid that the kingdom would destabilize if he left. To prevent future unrest, he ordered the executions of some of those who were responsible for the murders, as well as the arsonists. However, the number of punished people was small. He couldn't punish the whole population of London, and some of the perpetrators were of high social status. He issued an edict demanding that the Jews were to be left in peace. However, the edict was not properly enforced. In March, violence developed, and a massacre at York occurred.

Richard departed England in 1190, on his way to the Holy Land to fight Saladin. To finance this endeavor, he gathered money by raising taxes, implementing a Saladin tithe (a tax to aid freeing Jerusalem), selling his personal estates, and lending money. He was said to have declared he would sell London if he could find a buyer. Richard even forced those who held official positions to pay for them. If they declined, he would offer those positions to the highest bidders. Before departing, Richard appointed two regents over England: Hugh de Puiset, Bishop of Durham, and William de Mandeville, Earl of Essex. William de Mandeville soon died and was succeeded by William Longchamp. Richard's brother John was dissatisfied with his brother's decision and started plotting how to gain control over the throne.

On his way to the Holy Land, Richard met and betrothed Berengaria of Navarre, daughter of King Sancho VI of Navarre, the land that bordered Richard's Aquitaine. Marriage with Berengaria secured the borders of his duchy but angered Philip, king of France, who considered Richard betrothed to his own sister, Alys. Richard took his wife with him on a crusade, but they returned from the holy war separately. After the separation, Berengaria, Queen of England, never saw Richard again, and their marriage remained childless. She saw the kingdom for the first time after her husband's death.

During the Third Crusade, Richard fought and won many battles against Saladin, but he never managed to conquer Jerusalem. In 1191, he suffered from scurvy, but even ill, he fought by being carried. He was a forceful warrior skilled in the art of warfare, and for his courage, he earned the title Lionheart. Even Baha ad-Din, Saladin's biographer, mentions Richard's martial skills. In September of 1192, Richard and Saladin reached the truce that would secure a three-year peace and allow Richard to return home to deal with his brother John, who had been plotting with King Philip of France to overthrow him from England's throne.

While on his way back from the crusade, Richard shipwrecked near Aquileia in Italy. He was forced to continue his travels by land, through Central Europe. Near Vienna, he was captured by Leopold of Austria, who accused him of the murder of his cousin. Leopold also had a personal grudge against Richard, who had cast down his standard from the walls of Acre during the Third Crusade. Richard was then imprisoned at Dürnstein Castle in Austria. The regents of England did not know what happened to Richard for quite some time. It was illegal to imprison a crusader, and Pope Celestine III excommunicated Leopold for his behavior. In 1193, Richard was handed over to the Holy Roman Empire, which also imprisoned him. Holy Roman Emperor Henry VI was angry with Richard because he had given his support to Henry the Lion, a German duke who was in dispute with the emperor. He demanded ransom for Richard, as he needed the money to raise an army. For the wrongful containment of Richard, Henry VI was also excommunicated by Pope Celestine III. Richard's mother Eleanor worked to gather the ransom, which was 150,000 marks (100,000 pounds of silver). Silver and gold were confiscated from the churches, and all clergy had to pay taxes at the height of a quarter of the value of everything they owned. While Eleanor was gathering money to pay the ransom for Richard, his brother John and Philip of France offered 80,000 marks to Emperor Henry VI to keep Richard prisoner. Henry VI turned down the offer. Finally, on February 4, 1194, the ransom money reached Germany, and Richard was released.

To nullify the shame of his imprisonment, upon his return Richard was crowned for the second time as king of England. He forgave his brother's plotting with the French king and even declared John as his heir. While Richard was imprisoned, Philip had conquered Normandy, and Richard set out to regain it. Determined not only to regain Normandy but also to stop Philip from taking over other Angevin lands in France, Richard invested all his resources and military expertise in a war against France. Forming an alliance with his father-in-law Sancho VI of Navarre and Baldwin IX of Flanders, Richard won several victories over Philip. Philip fled, and Richard captured all of his financial assets.

One March evening, Richard was walking the perimeter of Chalus Chabrol Castle, which he had besieged. He was observing the castle walls, from which occasional missiles were shot. He was amused by one of the men on the walls, who used a frying pan instead of a shield to deflect missiles. At that moment, he got shot in the shoulder by a crossbow from another man on the wall. The wound quickly became gangrenous, and Richard was dying. He asked to see the man who shot him, but it turned out it was a boy who was fighting to avenge his family's death by Richard's soldiers. Instead of executing the boy, Richard forgave him and even gave him money to enjoy his newly earned freedom. Richard died on April 6, 1199, while being held by his mother. His heart was buried in Rouen, Normandy, his entrails in Chalus, and the rest of his body next to his father in Anjou.

It is unclear whether the boy who shot Richard enjoyed his freedom after the king's death. Some chroniclers claim he was captured and flayed alive by a mercenary captain who was in Richard's employment.

Before joining the Third Crusade, Richard made sure his brother John was satisfied enough with his position in the kingdom that he wouldn't try to usurp the throne. John was married to the wealthy Isabella, Countess of Gloucester, and enjoyed the privileges of lands such as Cornwall, Derby, Devon, Dorset, Nottingham, and Somerset. However, Richard kept the key castles in all these territories so that John was unable to rise in power and form his own army. All these preemptive measures did not stop John from acting as soon as his brother left on a crusade. He immediately clashed with Regent William Longchamp, and the hostility between the two quickly turned into an armed conflict. John had William locked up in the Tower of London, and people recognized him as Richard's heir, but the coming of Walter de Coutances, Archbishop of Rouen, undermined his plans. Walter was sent by Richard to deal with the situation in England, and he brought news of Richard's marriage with the princess of Navarre, which gave new hope of a possible child from this marriage that would be the rightful heir to the throne of England.

When Richard became imprisoned in Europe, John proclaimed him dead or otherwise lost, while he himself went to Paris to make an alliance with French King Philip. He promised to dispose of his wife Isabella and marry Philip's sister Alys in return for the king's support. Another armed conflict broke out in England between Richard's supporters and John's newly-acquired army. Richard finally returned to England in 1194 and proclaimed his brother John innocent of treason, as he was only a child acting on bad advice from malicious councilors, even though, at the time, John was twenty-seven. Officially proclaimed Richard's heir, John continued to support his brother until the end of his reign.

Richard's death in 1199 created yet another succession struggle. Even though Richard named John as his heir, another possibility for the throne's succession was his nephew Arthur, son of Geoffrey. The medieval laws were unclear about how to proceed with the two throne pretenders. Norman law was in favor of John because he was the only surviving son of King Henry II. However, Angevin law favored Arthur, as he was the son of Henry's elder son. War soon broke out, with John being crowned at Westminster Abbey in 1199. He had the support of English and Norman nobility, while Arthur had the support of French King Philip II. The conflict lasted until 1204 when John lost the Duchy of Normandy to King Philip II of France. This defeat made various chroniclers call John the Softsword, in contrast to his aggressive and always battle-ready brother Richard. John tried to retake Normandy during his entire reign. To pay the army and hire mercenaries for the endeavor, he had to collect money in ways that marked him as money-minded, extortionate, and miserly. During his reign, he raised taxes eleven times. By comparison, the previous three monarchs together raised taxes a total of eleven times. John also demanded payments be made to the royal treasury when a castle or estate was being inherited. Fines and penalties for crimes were increased, and John kept all the profit made through the justice system. He also raised taxes on widows who wished to remain single and not remarry, although this tax was Richard's invention. Jews were taxed highest of all, as they had the protection of the king himself. John didn't just elevate existing taxes; he also came up with a few of his own, such as new taxes on income and movable goods, as well as taxes on the import and export of the goods. The taxes were so high that many people simply couldn't pay them. In that case, the king would confiscate estates, castles, and land and sell them to the highest bidder, ensuring his profit. All this money-gathering didn't help him reconquer Normandy. In fact, it created tension between the Crown and the barons that later escalated into war.

In 1205, Hubert Walter, the Archbishop of Canterbury, died. John wanted to appoint John de Gray, Bishop of Norwich, as the new archbishop. However, the cathedral chapter (council of clergy) of Canterbury Cathedral claimed the right to appoint the archbishop's successor. They chose Reginald, the chapter's sub-prior, who secretly traveled to Rome to be confirmed as Archbishop of Canterbury by Pope Innocent III. To complicate the matter even more, the bishops of Canterbury province claimed they also had the right to appoint the archbishop, and they supported the king's choice of John de Gray. By king's orders, they sent a message to the pope about their decision. Pope Innocent III denied his support to both Reginald and appointee John de Gray. He had his own candidate for the position, Cardinal Stephen Langton, who he consecrated in 1207. John opposed the pope's decision and forbade Langton to enter England. In addition, he confiscated all archbishopric lands and other papal possessions in England. In return, Pope Innocent III placed an interdict on England in 1208. The clergy were strictly prohibited from performing any religious services except baptism for the young and absolutions for the dying.

John considered the interdict to be equal to a declaration of war. He seized the possessions of any clergy who obeyed the pope's interdict by refusing to hold services and promised protection for those who sided with him. Innocent III threatened to excommunicate John if he did not acknowledge Langton as archbishop and fulfilled this threat in 1209 when John showed himself too stubborn to comply. But John didn't care much about the excommunication. He continued to seize clergy properties and take a profit from their estates. Chroniclers note that John took fourteen percent of the church's total income on a yearly basis. The tension between John and Pope Innocent III continued and even escalated to the point that John was forced to agree to negotiations. John agreed to pay a feudal service to the papacy and compensate for the revenues the church had lost during the crisis. In return, Pope Innocent III became John's supporter until the end of his reign, both in domestic and foreign affairs. John never fully paid his debt to the church, and based on the lack of prosecution, it seems that the pope forgot about the debt, too.

The barons of the northern territories of England had little to do with John's efforts to reclaim Normandy but were in debt to the king since they were not able to pay the taxes imposed on them. Angered, northern barons organized a revolt described as "a rebellion of the king's debtors." Even John's military household joined the rebels, as their loyalty lay with their kinship ties, not with John. John's failure in France was probably the last straw that led to the armed conflict during John's final years of reign.

In 1215, John gathered a council to discuss reforms and sponsorship of negotiations with the rebelling barons. In the meantime, he gathered an army and even hired mercenaries in preparation for the uprising. To secure himself, he declared he would join the crusade, thus gaining certain protection from the church. Rebels appointed Robert FitzWalter as their military leader and renounced their debts and feudal ties to the king. The rebels named themselves the "Army of God" and marched on London, taking Lincoln and Exeter on their way. Once the rebels took London, John's army suffered a wave of defectors who joined the barons. The peace talks were held near Windsor Castle on June 15, 1215. Archbishop Langton was the mediator of the talks, and he created a charter that captured the proposed agreement. This charter would later be called the Magna Carta. The charter didn't address just the current uprising of the barons. It went further and proposed fundamental political reforms that included the rights of free men but not those of serfs and slaves. The Magna Carta promised swift justice, limitation of taxes, church rights, and protection from illegal imprisonment, among other points. A council of twenty-five barons was created to oversee John's commitment to the charter. After the negotiations, the rebel army was supposed to surrender London to the king. However, the barons didn't believe John would accept their council and refused to give up London. John asked the pope for support, and Innocent III obliged, declaring that the charter is shameful, demeaning, illegal, and unjust. He proceeded to excommunicate the rebel barons. The failure of the negotiations culminated in the First Barons' War.

Rebels were the first to attack, and they seized Rochester Castle, which was Langton's possession. The castle had an important strategic position. However, it did not help the rebels much. John was well prepared for the war since he had accumulated enough money to hire mercenaries for a planned invasion of France. The king owned a network of castles that isolated northern rebels from the southern rebels, so they could not join forces. At the same time, in Wales, Llywelyn the Great led an uprising, but John chose to ignore it for the time being. At the beginning of the campaign against the rebels, John was successful. He managed to retake Rochester Castle, and with a divided army, he reclaimed East Anglia, Northern London, and the estates of northern barons. Alexander II of Scotland allied himself with the rebels, as he claimed the right to the northern territories of England. In 1216, John reclaimed those territories from Alexander and even pushed further north towards Edinburgh. The response rebels prepared was to invite French Prince Louis to come to England and become their leader. Louis was married to the granddaughter of Henry II, and he had the right to claim the English throne through this marriage. King Philip refused to support his son in this endeavor, but he may have provided him with a private army. Louis landed in Kent, unopposed, in May of 1216. John planned to defend the English shores from the upcoming invasion, but his large fleet was dispersed due to heavy storms. Because of his open attack on English soil, Louis was excommunicated by Pope Innocent III. John was forced to retreat and reorganize his army. Louis took the opportunity and seized southeast England and parts of the north. Upon seeing the advancement of rebels, some of John's military household once again defected, including his half-brother William Longespée.

During the First Barons' War, John contracted dysentery, but he continued to fight. Luck was not on his side, and he started losing battles as his health deteriorated. John died on the night of October 18/19, 1216. He was buried in Worcester Cathedral, his body accompanied by mercenaries.

The civil war continued until the royal army gained a victory at the Battle of Lincoln in 1217. Louis gave up his claim to the English throne in favor of nine-year-old Henry III, John's son. The Magna Carta agreement was finally installed and became a basis for the future government.

# Chapter 10 – Late Middle Ages and the Black Death

Depiction of the spread of the Black Death

https://en.wikipedia.org/wiki/Black_Death#/media/File:1346-1353_spread_of_the_Black_Death_in_Europe_map.svg

The succession of Henry III, son of John of England, marks the beginning of the Late Middle Ages, which lasted until the beginning of the Tudor dynasty in 1485. In the history of England, this is also the period which marks the end of the medieval period and the start of the Renaissance.

Henry III was only nine years old when he was crowned in 1216 during the First Barons' War. William Marshal, First Earl of Pembroke, was chosen by the royal council to be Henry's protector and regent of the kingdom. He was loyal to the crown, as he had served four previous kings. Even though he was advanced in age, he became the leader of the royal armies in the Barons' War and ended it with the battles of Lincoln and Sandwich in 1217.

Henry III promised he would conform his rule to the Magna Carta, which greatly restricted royal authority. He spent much of his reign trying to restore that authority. However, only in 1220, with the help of the papacy, did he start reinforcing his power. He was then crowned for the second time, with new regalia, to confirm his authority as a king. Barons promised to return lands and castles they had taken during the civil war and to bow to the king because they were threatened with excommunication. In 1227, Henry was considered old enough to assume formal control over his kingdom. When William Marshal died in 1219, Henry was under the protection of the royal council. Hubert de Burgh became his closest advisor. To thank him for the service, Henry made him Earl of Kent and gave him a position as justiciar of the government for the remainder of his life.

The political power of Hubert de Burgh started declining in 1231 when his opponent Peter des Roches accused him of wasting royal money and lands. Henry III arrested Hubert and locked him in the Tower of London. Peter took over Henry's government and started seizing land from his opponents, completely ignoring the legal process. Powerful barons started complaining about Peter's actions, and a new civil war started in which Richard, the son of William Marshal, was leading the opposition. The fighting started in Ireland and South Wales, where Richard held some lands. He even offered his support to Welsh prince Llywelyn, who led his own rebellion against England. In 1234, the Archbishop of Canterbury intervened and mediated negotiations. Peace was achieved, although, in the meantime, Richard died of wounds received in battle.

During Henry III's rule, the word parliament was used for the first time, and it meant a gathering of the royal court, which had the power of decision over the matter of taxes. Henry ruled in accordance with the charters, which meant his power was limited, and his rule was constitutional. He was also very devoted to the church, with demonstrations of piety during public events. He invested heavily in religious causes and charity. He had papal support throughout his reign, and because of it, he often eagerly defended the mother church.

In 1258, Henry III faced a revolt of English barons. They were angered by the manner in which royal officials raised money, the influence of the French House of Lusignan on the court, the king's unpopular foreign politics, and the abuse of purchased Jewish loans by the royalty. Even Henry's wife, Queen Eleanor, secretly supported the revolting barons. Fearing that he would be arrested by the angered barons, Henry agreed to their terms of giving up his personal rule and governing through a council, which would be composed of barons and clergy. The only demand he had was that he get to choose half the people that would represent the council. Henry decided to choose the majority of his councilors from the hated House of Lusignan, which only deepened the discontent among the barons. The stability of England suffered as power swung back and forth between the king and the barons. While publicly supporting the Provisions of Oxford, a deal with the barons that reduced royal authority even more, Henry asked Pope Urban IV to absolve him from the oath. In 1261, Henry announced that the pope had released him from the promises he had made in the Provisions of Oxford. He then tried to retake all power over the kingdom. He had the support of his son and heir, Prince Edward.

Another civil war broke out in 1264, remembered as the Second Barons' War. Forces of rebelling barons were led by Simon de Montfort, while royal armies were initially led by Henry III. However, he gave full control to Prince Edward during the final stages of the war. Edward proved to be up to the task and won a victory at the Battle of Evesham, resulting in the death of Simon de Montfort. The rebellion, now leaderless, carried on for nearly two more years before the last of the rebels were captured on the Isle of Ely in 1267.

### The End of the House of Plantagenet

Upon the death of King Henry III, his eldest son Edward took the crown. Edward spent much of his reign rebuilding the royal administration and common law that regulated criminal and property laws. In later years of his rule, Edward responded to a rebellion in Wales (1282), which escalated to a full war of conquest. He was victorious and managed to subdue Wales under English rule and inhabit a series of castles in Wales with English people. After Wales, he turned his attention to Scotland, where he was invited to settle a succession dispute. Instead, he claimed feudal control over Scotland and started a war that would continue well after his death.

During the rule of King Edward I, Jews were expelled from the kingdom. Christians were forbidden from providing loans with interest, so Jews were the only ones who practiced the business. According to law, the king had the right to collect a tax from money-lending Jews, and if he wished to increase the tax, he did not need the approval of parliament. In 1275, Edward issued the Statute of the Jewry in response to a growing anti-Semitic movement in England. Under this statute, all usury was prohibited, and Jews were given fifteen years to buy land or pursue other professions. However, English people showed prejudice towards Jews and would not sell them land or accept them as students of skilled crafts. Hatred towards Jews grew, and King Edward issued the Edict of

Expulsion in 1290, which was widely accepted and quickly implemented.

In the autumn of 1290, Scotland lost its last heir to the throne, Princess Margaret, due to illness. Without the heir apparent, a crisis emerged, known in history as the "Great Cause." Edward was invited to settle the dispute, but he insisted that Scotland should recognize him as a feudal overlord. Scots did not like what Edward was proposing and instead formed an alliance with France. In response, Edward invaded Scotland in 1296 and installed an English government. However, Edward's triumph was temporary: in 1297, a new resistance emerged under the leadership of Andrew de Moray and William Wallace. The uprising in Scotland was treated as a rebellion of subjects of the English crown, not as a war between two nations. King Edward was extremely brutal in punishing the families of Scottish nobles and rebellion leaders. Edward died of dysentery in 1307, leaving the Scottish question unresolved.

Edward I was succeeded by his fourth son, Edward II, who ruled the Kingdom of England from 1307 until he was deposed in 1327. To ease the tensions between England and France, Edward II married Isabella, the daughter of King Philip IV of France. He also had a controversial relationship with Piers Gaveston, First Earl of Cornwall. It remains unknown in history whether they were lovers, sworn brothers, or just friends. It is this relationship that would cause tension between the king and the aristocracy, as well as with France, as Gaveston gathered more and more power and influence over the king. Edward was forced to exile Gaveston on more than one occasion, but he kept recalling him and restoring him to power. Upon one of the Gaveston's returns to England, barons forced Edward II to agree on reforms called the Ordinances of 1311, which significantly restricted royal powers. The barons, now having the power, banished Gaveston. This angered the king, who revoked the reforms and once again recalled his friend back to England. In 1312, a group of barons led by the Earl of Lancaster captured

Gaveston and murdered him, which caused armed conflict with the king. Edwards's forces had to return to Scotland, where Robert the Bruce, king of Scotland, defeated Edward at the Battle of Bannockburn in 1314. After being defeated by the Scots, Edward was forced to reinstall the Ordinances of 1311. At that time, a wide phenomenon known as the Great Famine, in which agriculture failed to feed the population of the kingdom due to weather instability, spread into the territory of England from northern Europe.

Edward II was directly blamed for the famine, and strong criticism of his rule culminated with a civil war in 1321. This civil war was known as the Despenser War, named after the Despenser family, who became extremely close to the king and started accumulating power. There was also opposition from the Earl of Lancaster, who had the support of other barons. After many battles, the Earl of Lancaster was captured at Boroughbridge and taken to Pontefract Castle, where a brief trial was held. He was found guilty and executed.

Edward II's marriage started to deteriorate due to his friendship with the Despensers. Advised by Hugh Despenser the Younger, Edward seized the lands of barons who had property in Scotland—among them the Beaumonts, close friends of his wife. Isabella also blamed Hugh for the arrest of her household when her children were taken away and placed in Hugh's wife's care. When she was sent to France to negotiate with her brother, King Charles, she refused to return to England. She had gotten involved in a relationship with the exiled lord, Roger Mortimer, and they joined forces to expel Edward and the Despensers from the English throne. Soon after, Isabella was joined by her son, Prince Edward. The alliance carefully planned an invasion of England.

In September of 1326, Roger Mortimer, Queen Isabella, Prince Edward, and the king's half-brother Edmund of Woodstock landed in Orwell, where they met no resistance. They were joined by enemies of the Despensers: Edwards's second half-brother Thomas of Brotherton, Henry of Lancaster, and a range of other barons and clergymen. During the invasion, Edward II's authority over the Kingdom of England collapsed, and Isabella took control over the administration with the support of the church. Hugh Despenser was executed, but the king's position proved to be problematic, as he was still married to Isabella. The procedure for removing a king did not exist in England until that point. It was up to parliament to decide the future fate of the powerless king, and they decided to remove and replace him with his son, Edward III. The king abdicated in favor of his son on January 21, 1327.

Edward III was crowned in February of 1327 and ruled until his death in 1377. He is remembered as a great military strategist and for restoring the royal authority his father had lost during his disastrous rule. His reign was long; he ruled for fifty years and witnessed the Black Death and the evolution of the English Parliament. He also started a war with France, known as the Hundred Years' War, by proclaiming himself the rightful heir of the French throne in 1337. Due to his inactivity in politics, the later years of his reign are remembered by failure in international relations as well as by domestic conflicts.

## The Black Death: The Greatest Catastrophe

Medieval portrayal of a plague doctor

https://en.wikipedia.org/wiki/Black_Death#/media/File:Paul_F%C3%BCrst,_Der_Doctor_Schnabel_von_Rom_(coloured_version).png

The Black Death was a pandemic of a plague that affected most of Eurasia. It devastated Europe and the Middle East from 1346 until 1353. It was the most devastating pandemic in history, as it is estimated to have claimed the lives of anywhere between seventy-five million to 200 million people. It took 200 years for the population of Europe to recover its numbers. The cause of the plague was a bacterium known as *Yersinia pestis*, carried by the rat fleas that inhabited trade ships. The bacterium can cause several types of plagues, but it was the bubonic plague that had the most severe manifestation throughout England. Newer research proves that, at that time, this strain of the bacterium was newly-evolved. Because of this, humans had not developed immunity against it, which explains its easy passage and virulence, as well as its high death rates.

The origins of the Black Death were in Central Asia, where the bacterium *Yersinia pestis* is endemic. It is believed that, due to climate change and drought in Asia, rodents started fleeing the dry grasslands and inhabiting highly-populated cities, where the disease could spread among humans. It is not known if the plague traveled to Europe with Mongol armies and traders via the Silk Road, or if it was brought by ships.

The most common symptom of bubonic plague is the appearance of buboes (for which it was named) mainly in the groin area, under the arms, and on the neck. Buboes, caused by inflammation of the lymph nodes, swell up and ooze pus and blood if opened. Fever and vomiting were also common symptoms of bubonic plague, as well as black spotting over the body, and rashes. Death would follow two to seven days after the initial infection.

Although the name "Black Death" was coined by the Belgian astronomer Simon de Covino in 1350, the term was not used widely before a 17th-century Danish historian used the phrase. Contemporary chroniclers were calling it either the "Great Plague" or the "Great Pestilence." The Black Death reached England in 1348, and its first known victim was a sailor who arrived in Dorset from the English province of Gascony. It took only one year for the disease to spread through the whole kingdom. New estimations, which are widely accepted, give the figure of a forty to sixty percent death rate in England alone.

Right before the Black Plague, the Kingdom of England was developing into a major military power of Europe due to the politics of King Edward III. In 1346, England won the Battle of Neville's Cross with the Scots, and it even seemed that Edward would fulfill his father's wish and implement English suzerainty over Scotland. In the same year, the English king was victorious against the French royal armies in the Battle of Crécy, where Edward led his numerically inferior army. The Great Famine of 1315-17 had already reduced the English population, but it is not known how many people inhabited England right before the Black Death occurred. Ninety percent of the kingdom was agricultural and inhabited villages, but London had around 70,000 inhabitants, followed by Norwich with its 12,000 people. Today's estimation is that the Black Death took the lives of three to seven million people in England.

Historians agree that the first occurrence of the plague was in Dorset, but many sources dating from the same period mention Southampton or Bristol as the place of origin. It is possible that the plague arrived in those places independently. From Dorset, the disease spread quickly over the southwestern parts of the kingdom. Bristol was the first city that was affected by the disease, and London was reached in autumn of 1348. The countryside was last to suffer, but it did not evade the pandemic. There are three possible routes by which the plague traveled to London: overland from Dorset through Winchester, overland from Gloucester, or along the coastline by ship. In big, overcrowded cities with narrow streets and poor house ventilation, conditions were nearly perfect for the spead of the plague. The Black Death spread north during the first half of 1349. The plague arrived by ship at the Humber estuary and started spreading both north and south; the north was ravaged during the summer months.

The plague spreads during warm weather, as *Yersinia pestis* bacteria cannot survive temperatures below forty-two degrees Fahrenheit (six degrees Celsius). In December of 1349, the plague started dying down in England, and life slowly returned to normal.

The bubonic plague is still present in some areas of the world, and if diagnosed in time, it is treatable with the help of antibiotics. However, during the Middle Ages, antibiotics were not known, and those who practiced medicine used some of the more violent approaches to treating the disease: forced vomiting, sweating, and bloodletting. Bloodletting was extremely popular in the early stages of the disease, while swelling of the lymph nodes was mild. It included opening a vein on the ankle or wrist on the same side of the body where the swelling appeared. Sweating was reserved for the last stages of the disease, and it was induced by bezoar water, serpentary rhizome (snakeroot), or similar remedies. The concept behind this treatment was to purge the corruption of the disease through the violent sweating of the patient, who would also be wrapped in a wet blanket.

# Chapter 11 – The Hundred Years' War

The great battles of the Hundred Years' War, beginning from the top left: La Rochelle, Agincourt, Patay, Orleans.

https://en.wikipedia.org/wiki/Hundred_Years%27_War#/media/File:Hundred_years_war_collage.jpg

A series of conflicts between England and France, famously known as the Hundred Years' War, in fact lasted for 116 years, between 1337 and 1453. Rulers of England's House of Plantagenet were fighting the French royal House of Valois over the right to rule France. France and England had been constantly under tense relations since the Normans had invaded England and started ruling it. Normans were French in origin, and while they gained new titles on the soil of England, they kept their old French territories. They were kings of England as well as dukes of Normandy and later Anjou, Brittany, Gascony, etc. French royalty always tried to diminish the power of English kings in its territories, and Normandy was an attractive prize. Whenever England was at war or under civil unrest, French kings would seize the opportunity to invade English holdings in France. By the beginning of the 14th century, only Gascony remained as English property. The English royal house constantly tried to regain those territories, especially Normandy and Anjou, but to no avail–until King Edward III of England, who started the Hundred Years' War.

In 1316, France denied women any succession rights. Therefore, when Charles IV of France died in 1328, leaving no son or brothers as heir, France experienced a succession crisis. The closest male relative of the deceased king was Edward III of England, the son of Charles' sister Isabella. Isabella tried to claim the right to the French throne for her son. However, France rejected her, citing the law that dictated she had no succession rights and could not, therefore, transmit them to her son. Eventually, French aristocracy settled and chose a patrilineal cousin of Charles, Philip VI, as king of France. He was the first king of the newly established House of Valois. The English seemed satisfied with the choice and did not press the matter of their right to the succession. However, later political disagreements between Philip VI and Edward III led to a conflict in which the English king re-opened the question of succession and tried to claim his right to the French crown.

Edward III formally assumed the title "King of France and the French Royal Arms" in 1340, and in the same year, he received homage from Guy, the Count of Flanders' brother. The cities of Ghent, Ypres, and Bruges recognized Edward as king of France. He gained alliances with Netherlands, Belgium, and Flanders, all of which supported his claim to the French throne and considered him the true king of France. The English king was ready for an invasion of France.

In the summer of 1340, the English fleet was ready to set sail, and they landed on the French coast on June 22. However, the French fleet was ready and waiting at the port of Sluys. The English were victorious in the first naval battle and kept dominance over the English Channel during the whole course of the war, preventing a possible invasion of the English kingdom. The war would have ended here, as Edward's funds were exhausted, but the Duke of Brittany died suddenly, and another succession crisis began. There were two possible heirs to the Duke of Brittany: the deceased duke's half-brother John of Montfort and Charles of Blois, who had been married in the old duke's house. French King Philip VI gave his support to Charles, who was also the king's nephew. John of Montfort had the support of English King Edward III. The War of the Breton Succession started and would last until 1365.

The war between France and England came to a halt during the Black Death in 1348 but resumed by 1355. England recovered financially and launched another attack on France. The attack was led by Edward III's son, Edward the Prince of Wales, who would become known as the Black Prince due to his black armor. The prince had a series of victories, but he failed to take Bourges. France had a new king, John II, also known as John the Good, and the two briefly negotiated. However, no truce was achieved. The fighting continued, and, in 1356, King John II was captured and held hostage, together with his son Louis of Anjou, other nobles and citizens of Paris, and representatives from nineteen principal towns of France. His son, Charles V, immediately assumed the role of regent, and the first peace treaty between England and France, the Treaty of Brétigny, marked the end of the first phase of the Hundred Years' War in 1360.

England asked for a ransom of three million crowns and released King John II, whose task was to collect the money. In the meantime, the French prince, Louis of Anjou managed to escape, and King John II felt honor-bound to return to captivity. His motives to return to captivity might also have been an unwillingness to escalate the conflict further. John II died in captivity in England and was succeeded by his son, Charles V, in 1364.

The second phase of the Hundred Years' War is known as the Caroline War. Once again, it began over a succession dispute, this time in the Kingdom of Castile. French King Charles V managed to depose Peter the Cruel from the throne of Castile in revenge for poisoning his sister-in-law, although political reasons are not to be ignored. Charles supported Henry of Trastámara, who became ruler of Castile after Peter the Cruel and agreed on an alliance with France. This alliance provided the French king with the naval support he needed to launch an invasion in England. In the Battle of La Rochelle in 1372, the Castilian fleet defeated the English. The English counterattack, led by John de Montfort, Duke of Brittany, was initially successful. While progressing further down the south of France, the English encountered more and more resistance. Charles V ordered French forces to avoid open battle with the English forces. However, the French continued to surround the English army shadowing them, and by October 1373, the English were completely trapped against the River Allier, as French forces encircled them on all four sides. The English were lucky and managed to cross the river; however, they lost all their supplies and horses. English soldiers were falling ill and starving, but in December, they finally reached friendly territory in Gascony. Their march across France, although a magnificent achievement, was a complete military failure.

In England, both the Black Prince and his father, King Edward III, were ill. The Black Prince died in 1376, King Edward III a year later. The English throne was succeeded by Richard II, son of the Black Prince. However, he was still a ten-year-old child. To avoid Richard's uncle John of Gaunt usurping the throne, the English parliament decided Richard II would rule not with a regent, but with the help of a series of councils. Richard was an unpopular king, as he tried to raise taxes to pay for the conflict with the Scots and for the Peasants' Revolt that occurred in 1381.

In 1380, France also lost its king, who was succeeded by his son Charles VI, at the age of eleven. He ruled with the help of his regent uncles, who continued the war with England. Taxes were to be raised all over France to finance the war; however, the citizens were unwilling to pay them. In 1382, Charles VI also faced revolts from the citizens. The war slowed down as both kingdoms had to deal with their domestic affairs. The kingdoms did continue to fight through proxy wars, mainly during the Portuguese interregnum of 1383-1385, during which Portugal had no ruler.

Unlike the English nobility, Richard II showed disinterest in continuing the war with France. The lords who wanted to continue the war made an alliance led by Richard's uncle Thomas of Woodstock. The alliance, known by the name Lords Appellant, gained control over the royal council in 1388. However, the alliance was unsuccessful in reigniting the war due to a lack of funds. In autumn of the same year, the council decided to start negotiations with the French, and the result was a three-year truce at Leulinghem. Over the next few years, Richard II reasserted his authority in England and exiled the son of one of his uncles, Henry of Bolingbroke. But in the same year, Henry returned to England and gathered supporters who helped him depose Richard and crown himself Henry IV, King of England.

During the three-year peace, Henry IV concentrated on resolving the issues with the Scots, who continued to attack England's northern borders. After the Battle of Homildon Hill, where the Scots were defeated, and issue arose between the king and First Earl of Northumberland, Henry Percy. The struggle over the lands gained in the war against the Scots was bloody and long. It resulted in the complete destruction of the Percy family in 1408.

In Wales, a new rebellion against English authority arose under the leadership of Welsh Prince Owain Glyndwr, who was crowned in 1400. Five years later, the Welsh allied themselves with France, which already had the support of Castile. The allied army invaded English territories and advanced as far as Worcester, the Castilian fleet raiding and burning from Cornwall to Southampton. The rebellion was put down in 1415, however. The result was Welsh semi-independence that lasted for a few years.

During this period, France faced civil war. King Charles VI descended into madness, and the long fight over the regency between his uncles and his brother escalated in open war conflict. The matter was resolved in 1418 when Burgundians took over Paris, and John the Fearless took over the regency.

Having no basis for open conflict, England and France continued fighting by creating and hiring pirates. English pirates operated mainly in the English Channel, while French pirates, under the protection of their allies, the Scots, raided English shores. Because of the domestic difficulties in both France and England, open war was halted for a decade.

Henry IV died in 1413 and was succeeded by his eldest son, Henry V, who ruled until his death in 1422. It was Henry V who was immortalized in Shakespeare's plays, commonly known as the "Henriads." He is still known as one of the greatest warrior kings of England. Henry V was the second king from the House of Lancaster, and his campaigns in France are known as the

Lancastrian War, the third and last phase of the Hundred Years' War.

In 1419, Henry V made an alliance with Philip the Good, son of John the Fearless, who took over Paris. Together, they forced the mad French King Charles VI to sign the Treaty of Troyes. By this treaty, Henry was obliged to marry Charles' daughter, Catherine of Valois, which would give him the regency and the right to inherit the French throne. The son of King Charles VI, Charles Dauphin, was disinherited. The Dauphin responded by proclaiming himself his father's regent and seizing royal authority. He continued to disobey his father's orders and established his own court at Bourges. Both English King Henry V and French King Charles VI died in 1422. Henry V had one son, who became King Henry VI of England. According to the Treaty of Troyes, Henry VI had the right to claim the throne of France. However, a baby King Henry (less than one at the time) had no support from the Armagnac political party of France, which was loyal to Charles Dauphin. Thus, the war continued. The following five years were marked with English victory that spread its territories in France from the English Channel to the Loire, and from Brittany to Burgundy.

During the Lancastrian phase of the war, France found a hero in Joan of Arc, the daughter of a farmer. She claimed to have received visions from the Archangel Michael, Saint Margaret, and Saint Catherine of Alexandria, who gave her instructions to seek Charles VII and support him, as only then would he expel the English from France and take the throne. She was sent to Orleans as part of the relief army where she got the nickname "The Maid of Orleans." Joan of Arc raised the morale of the French troops, who managed to defeat the English and make them lift their siege of the city. Inspired by Joan and this victory, the French army had a streak of victories. Charles was finally crowned as king of France in Reims in 1429. However, Joan was captured on May 23, 1430, while participating in the Battle at Compiègne. Her capturers were

French, a Burgundian faction of nobles who joined the English. Pro-English Bishop Pierre Cauchon put her on trial, mainly for heresy, but other charges were also included. Joan was found guilty and executed on May 30, 1431, by burning.

When the Duke of Bedford died in 1435, Burgundy lost interest in the alliance with England. The Duke of Burgundy signed the Treaty of Arras with King Charles VII of France. This treaty restored Paris to the French king and was a sign of the decline of English dominance in the Hundred Years' War. The French retook Rouen in 1449, and English forces started suffering defeats in various battles. The last battle of the Hundred Years' War was the Battle of Castillon, fought in 1453, in which a small Anglo-Gascon army attacked a French army encampment but failed to do any damage. Small conflicts continued to break out throughout the next twenty years, but the English had no resources to continue fighting the war; however, the Treaty of Picquigny in 1475 formally ended the war. Back home, agitated by the financial losses during the war with France, English landowners started complaining, which would lead to domestic unrest and the War of the Roses in 1455.

During the Hundred Years' War, England was deprived of all its continental possessions except Calais, a port city in northern France. The loss of the war had a profound effect on English society, which started to feel hostility towards anything French. In 1362, the English language became the official language of the kingdom, which meant that even kings and nobles resented French.

# Chapter 12 - War of the Roses, the End of an Age

The white rose of the House of York (left), and the red rose of the House of Lancaster (right)

https://en.wikipedia.org/wiki/Wars_of_the_Roses

The War of the Roses is a series of civil wars in England that concluded the medieval period. Two rival branches of the House of Plantagenet fought for the right of succession, as King Henry VI did not yet have an heir with his wife Margaret of Anjou. One was the House of York, whose emblem was a white rose, and the other was the House of Lancaster, with the emblem of a red rose. Because of the respective emblems, in the 19$^{th}$ century, this series of civil wars were united under the name Wars of the Roses. Upon the victory of Henry VII of the House of Tudor, the roses were combined to symbolize the unification of the two houses, thus creating what would later be known as the Tudor Rose.

Just like his grandfather, French King Charles VI, Henry VI showed signs of mental instability. Because of his deteriorating health, English nobles started fighting for power and influence over the easily-manipulated king. Feudal nobles hired private armies against each other, and conflict was imminent. However, in 1453, before Prince Edward was even born, Henry suffered a complete mental collapse and failed to respond to the birth of his son. The Great Council was quickly gathered, and Richard of the House of York declared himself its leader. By 1455, Henry regained his composure and, under the influence of Queen Margaret, banished Richard from the court. Margaret became the de facto leader of the House of Lancaster, and she gathered an alliance of nobles against Richard of York. About to face accusations of treason, Richard feared for his safety. He gathered an army and started open conflict in 1455.

The first battle of the Wars of Roses was fought at St Albans on May 22, 1455, when Richard led his forces to London but was intercepted by Henry's army. The result of the battle was the defeat of the House of Lancaster and the death of the allied lords of Northumberland and Somerset. The Yorkist army found King Henry VI hiding in a tanner's shop, completely abandoned by his allies, advisors, and servants. The king was indisposed, having another mental break down, and Margaret was charged with taking care of him. Richard resumed his position of influence in the Great Council, naming himself the Lord Protector of the kingdom. However, King Henry VI recovered by 1456 and once more relieved Richard of York from the duty of protector. Margaret wasn't satisfied with this decision and urged the king to revoke Richards's titles and reduce him to his previous position of lieutenant in Ireland. The fighting continued. In the Battle of Wakefield (1460), Lancastrians were victorious, and Richard of

York was killed during the fighting. His son, Edward of March, who was 18 years old, succeeded him as Earl of York. Edward continued his father's endeavors and led the Yorkist army in the next conflicts with the House of Lancaster.

Edward's goal was quite different than his father's. He did not want to be just Lord Protector of the kingdom and to advise Henry VI; he wanted to depose the king completely and take the crown for himself. Edward even had the support of the populace of London. He led his army to London, where he was received with welcome. Margaret had to flee, taking refuge for herself and Henry VI in the court of Scottish King James III. Edward was crowned in June 1461 and became Edward IV, King of England, with the lavish support of the people. Queen Margaret did not give up on the throne and continued her efforts as a leader of the House of Lancaster. In the Battle of Tewkesbury in 1471, her son Prince Edward was killed. With no son to inherit the throne, King Henry VI was murdered shortly after his son's death. The remaining years of Edward IV's rule were peaceful. However, he died suddenly in 1483, and succession turmoil followed once again. At the time, Edward's son was only twelve years old, and the nobles who opposed the king saw the young prince as unfit to rule. Edward had named his brother Richard as Lord Protector, but he was far in the north when the king died. To come to London, he needed to gather an army, as he was aware that the opposition would seize the opportunity to overthrow him. He also proclaimed his brother's marriage with Queen Elizabeth Woodville illegitimate. Therefore his heir, Prince Edward, could not be crowned. Richard claimed the throne for himself and was crowned Richard III.

The Duke of Buckingham organized opposition to Richard's rule and started a revolt in the southern territories of England. The duke did not give his support to Prince Edward or one of his siblings, who were secretly killed. Instead, he was supporting a Tudor. This might mean he already knew of the death of Edward's children. The Lancastrian claim on the throne was through the descendants of the half-brother to Henry VI, the First Earl of Richmond. Buckingham's uprising failed, but it wasn't the end of the plotting against Richard III. Buckingham's supporters created an alliance with Henry Tudor, who was in exile in France at the time. In France, Henry was given support and an army, which he led to England, where some of Richard's officers joined him or decided to be neutral and not fight the invading army in August of 1485. At the Battle of Bosworth, Henry defeated Richard III, who was killed in the fighting. The Battle of Bosworth was the last significant battle in the Wars of the Roses, and it marked the end not only of the power struggle for the English throne but also of the Middle Ages in England. Henry was crowned and became King Henry VII on August 22, 1485. He was the first king of the House of Tudor and the last king to win his crown on the battlefield.

With the end of the Middle Ages, England embarked into a new era of change. Power shifted from the feudal nobility to the ever-growing class of merchants. Under the Tudors, the kingdom moved towards a centralized monarchy and renaissance, which would bring great leaders and events, such as Henry VIII and the reformation of religion in England.

# Part 2: Magna Carta

*A Captivating Guide to the History of the Great Charter and its Influence on Medieval England and the Rest of the World*

# Introduction

The Magna Carta is celebrated as one of the most important documents in human history. It is the main source of constitutional law around the world, promising people liberties and protection from the arbitrary power of the government. However, it is also a set of promises extorted in bad faith from an unwilling king, and these promises dealt with the problems of the 13th-century aristocracy. Among the ordinary problems of fees, customs, and land law, greater ideas found their way into the document, revolutionary ideas that would change the world. However, in 1215, they were sparse, mentioned here and there in the form of high ideals more than in the form of a law.

Some parts of the Magna Carta are still quoted, such as clauses that deal with justice before peers, freedom from unlawful imprisonment, freedom of the church, and so on. However, in medieval times, these clauses did not have the same meaning as they do today. The Magna Carta showed itself to be a flexible document with ideas that could be bent and transformed to suit the needs of the new times.

The role of the Magna Carta in 1215 wasn't so much to grant freedoms to the citizens of the English Kingdom. It was a tool that would pin down a king and stop him from using excessive power to tax his own people or take away baronial possessions at his royal whim. When observed in the light of the medieval times from which it sprouted, the Magna Carta ought to be dead, remembered only by history and scholars. Instead, it is very much alive today, and it is even celebrated as the most hallowed document ever to be written. Numerous countries have based their constitutional laws upon the Magna Carta and admire it as the foundation of Western liberties, democracy, and the rule of law.

For all those who wonder, this book offers the answers to how events leading up to and following the penning of this important document unfolded. Starting with the background story of the unjust rule of King John, this book tells of the birth of the Magna Carta, its failure, its resurrection, and its transformation into the laws of today.

# Chapter 1 – King John

John was the youngest son of Henry II, King of England. As such, he was named "Lackland" because he couldn't possibly inherit any lands that were under the rule of his father. However, he was the favorite son, and Henry even considered naming him his successor. This would cause unrest within the kingdom, and the throne was passed to John's older brother, King Richard. John tried, unsuccessfully, to raise a rebellion against the rule of his brother while Richard was fighting in the Third Crusade. Upon his return to England, Richard made peace with John and even named him his successor. As Richard had no children, John inherited the throne and was crowned king in 1199. He became the ruler of England, Normandy, Anjou, Maine, Touraine, and Aquitaine– territories that historians often refer to as the Angevin Empire even though, officially, it was a kingdom. The territories ruled by the Angevins made up the largest landmass in Europe governed by a single ruler.

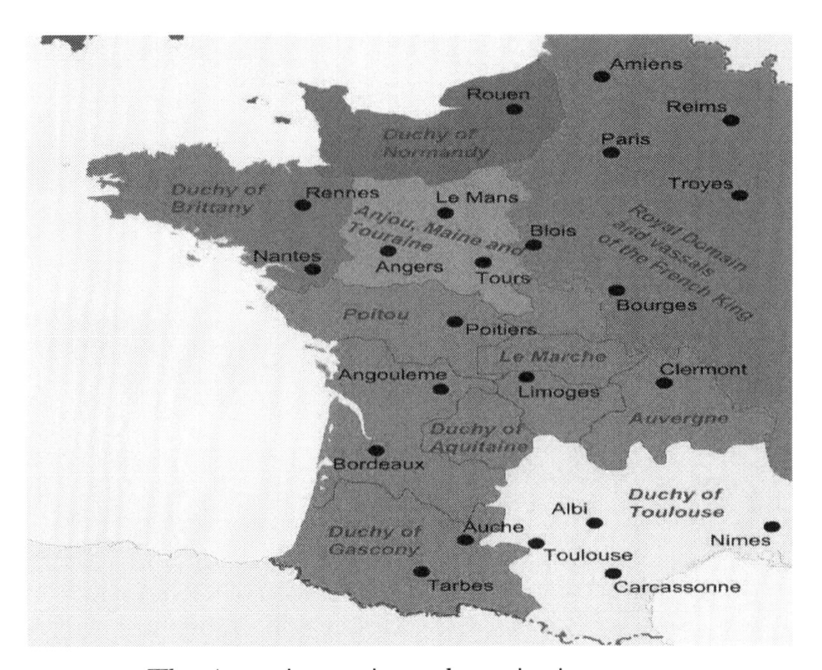


The Angevin continental empire in orange

(Source:https://en.wikipedia.org/wiki/John,_King_of_England#/media/File:Angevin_empire.svg)

During his first five years of rule, John lost the continental part of the Angevin Empire. His unwillingness to fight, and the fact that he often ran away from battle, earned him a new nickname: among his troops, he was known as John the "Softsword." His main enemy was Philip II, King of France, whose life goal was the destruction of Angevin rule in the French territories. Philip II was an excellent politician, a ruthless ruler, and he had a great appetite for power. He expanded the territories of the Kingdom of France, taking back provinces previously conquered by English kings. He even conquered the Duchy of Normandy, ancestral territory of the Angevin kings, striking a tremendous blow to King John.

John managed to quickly recover from all the losses in France. In 1206, England and France established a truce, and John turned his attention to governing England. The war with France was a disaster for the economy, and the king needed money. John raised taxes on everyone. Even the church was forced to contribute. Nobles, townsmen, and Jews were all pressed into paying unreasonable taxes. John was so successful in collecting the wealth that, by 1212, he had accumulated over £130,000 (about $200 million) in coins, which he hid in various castles that acted as royal treasuries.

A great deal of the gathered treasure caused John's conflict with the church because he was confiscating church lands and selling them to the nobles. This conflict arose when the Archbishop of Canterbury, Thomas Becket, died. The king used his authority to proclaim his own man, a bishop of Norwich's successor, to the position. Pope Innocent III had a different idea. He did not like John's idea of the king's authority over the church. John wasn't the only ruler of England to claim authority over the church; in fact, they all did. Even the most pious and religious William the Conqueror believed in state power over religion. This everlasting conflict would eventually lead to the separation of the English church during the rule of Henry VIII in the 16th century.

Pope Innocent III was determined to appoint a friend from his young student days, Stephen Langton, as the new Archbishop of Canterbury. King John opposed Langton for several reasons. He wanted his own man in the crucial religious position, and he did not trust Langton because he was schooled in Paris. Also, his brother was employed by Philip II of France for the same position in the French Notre Dame. John saw Langton as a politically inappropriate person for the position of archbishop in England. However, Pope Innocent convinced the delegation of the Christ Church in Canterbury to elect Langton as the new archbishop even though John objected with passion. In retaliation, he started confiscating church properties, thus escalating the conflict between the church and the state. To punish England for the confiscated lands, Pope Innocent imposed severe ecclesiastical penalties throughout the country. In 1208, he laid an interdict on England that prevented its church officials from performing certain religious rights and services. In 1209, he personally excommunicated John, seeing that the king wouldn't back down and give up the cause. John decided his financial gains from this conflict would, by far, surpass the risks he was taking with his immortal soul. In fact, the financial gain from the interdict is estimated to be around £60,000 (about $100 million), which was equal to two years' gross annual revenue.

With a rich royal treasury and a firm grip on his rule in England, John started concentrating on expanding his kingdom. However, this time he did not look toward France because he knew he had no chance to regain the lost territories there. Instead, he concentrated on the Celtic lands–Ireland, Wales, and Scotland. He disciplined the Anglo-Irish barons and reinforced his rule in their lands, thus conquering north Wales. In addition, he invaded Scotland, where he gained control over succession rights.

During King John's Welsh expedition, a plot against his life and his rule was brewing. The barons of England were planning to assassinate him and replace him with Simon de Montfort, the leader of the Albigensian Crusade, a war against the Cathars in southern France. John learned about this plot on August 16th, two days after the mass hanging of Welsh hostages, which had the purpose of shocking the rebellious citizens of Wales. Afraid for his life, the king abandoned the Welsh expedition and demanded hostages from rebelling barons be sent to the court. John suspected everyone and wouldn't leave his chambers without an armed escort. He bullied his opponents to the extent that two of the important barons, Robert Fitzwalter and Eustace de Vesci, fled to France and joined the forces of King Philip II. However, soon after the initial shock, John reversed his policies and started treating his opponents with more respect. In truth, the king hoped to convince some of the barons to support him. Instead, his strength as a ruler collapsed, and he was thereafter seen as a weak, desperate king whose failures and despotic rule angered the barons.

The English barons were the ones who benefitted the most from the conquest of the French territories by the previous kings. Consequently, their loss was tremendous when John lost all the continental territories. Their castles and lands were now owned by the French king, who had the right to give them to his own nobles. This meant that the English barons lost their source of income, a fact about which they could not be indifferent. It wasn't just the income the barons were worried about, however. Just as kings, they were ambitious men who sought to transfer their titles and territories to their heirs and marry their sons and daughters into well-established dynasties that would bring them riches and political security. Losing the French territories, the barons were unable to pay their debt to King John, and their English lands were seized. The first to be forfeited for non-payment of debt in 1207 was the Earldom of Leicester. In the following year, the lands of John's favorite, William de Braose (or de Briouze), followed. William was exiled, and his wife and son became John's prisoners. It is generally believed the two of them were starved to death while locked away in Windsor Castle. John interpreted the existing laws, and he took the liberty to come up with new ones as he saw fit. He tried to excuse himself by explaining that he was merely punishing those who did not pay their debts to the Crown. However, the barons had their own interpretation of the laws, and they saw John's rule as atrocious. To them, it seemed the king had too much power and had to be stopped.

In France, Fitzwalter and Vesci found sympathy with King Philip II and the papal legates. They complained about John's rule and attacked him personally, telling stories of John's infidelity, in which he took married women–mostly of noble origins–as his mistresses. It is not clear whether these stories were true or simply the fabrications of barons who sought support from the French court, yet John is remembered for his infidelity. The barons told the papal legate Pandulf Verraccio of their decision to rebel against the English king due to the interdict he brought upon his own country.

They also said they could not serve a king who was excommunicated. Fitzwalter and Vesci gained allies in addition to King Philip and the Vatican legates. They also gained support from exiled Englishmen who sought refuge in France, such as Giles de Braose (son of William de Braose), the Bishop of Hereford, and Stephen Langton.

John had two separate oppositions to his rule: the barons and the Vatican. Until the events in Paris, these two sides of the opposition were distant from each other. With Philip II acting as a mediator, however, the barons and the Vatican began to work together and were unified against a common enemy, the King of England. John was aware of this unification, and he tried to break them apart by making a deal with the pope. On May 15, 1213, at Ewell near Dover, the king formally surrendered the kingdom of England to the papal legate Pandulf. At the same time, he planned a new invasion of France, with which he tried to satisfy his supporters and gain new allies in alienated barons. However, the French, with their Flemish allies, defeated John's army on July 24, 1214, at the battle of Bouvines. Consequently, John promised Pope Innocent III that he would restore the lands of his main baronial opponents, Fitzwalter and Vesci. King John was defeated not only in battle but also in diplomacy. The worst blow he took was the exhaustion of his royal treasuries. Without money, he could not defend himself against his political enemies. He was naked in front of the opposition, and they had no reason to spare him.

# Chapter 2 – The Path to Runnymede

In October 1214, John was back in England from his failed French expedition, where he was immediately faced with the revolt of the taxpayers. The empty royal treasure demanded higher taxes once again, which the citizens could not bear. Accordingly, the opposition at home started taking its shape and structure. The moment was perfect since the leaders of the opposition, Fitzwalter, and Vesci, were back. As they were the first to be suspected of revolt, the two nobles were forced to change their strategy.

Typically, a revolt against a king had in mind a suitable replacement that would occupy the throne. In John's case, there was no suitable replacement. He made sure to get rid of every potential successor to the crown, and his own children were simply too young to pose a threat. Fitzwalter, Vesci, and other barons could not allow themselves to be rebels without a cause. The solution was to rebel not against the king but against his idea of how he should rule. They devised a set of legal and governmental reforms that would restrict the king's power and grant themselves a set of new liberties. These reforms were embodied in the form of a charter, which later the king would recognize as the Great Charter of the Liberties.

A new name rose in the English political scene of the 13th century–Stephen Langton. Langton was appointed the Archbishop of Canterbury in 1207. After his delayed appointment as archbishop, Langton swore fealty to King John, who at first opposed his installment in Canterbury. The pope instructed Langton to do everything in his power to bring peace to the king and to the kingdom. This meant he would be expected to behave as a mediator between two opposing sides, the king and the revolting barons. In 1213, the archbishop lifted the king's excommunication, and John, in return, swore to protect the kingdom and the church. He also swore to maintain the favorable laws and get rid of the unjust ones, as well as to provide justice for everyone equally. However, the barons were free to interpret the oath of their king as they wished, and they claimed it meant the restoration of ancient baronial liberties. They invoked the Coronation Charter of Henry I, which would allow the barons to enjoy the rights that John had managed to take from them. This charter was meant to bind the king to treating nobles, church officials, and individuals in accordance with the law. The over-taxation of the barons was condemned by the charter, as well as any form of corruption. However, the Coronation Charter of Henry I was ignored by the king until 1213. Rumor has it that Langton himself reminded the barons of this charter and their guaranteed rights; however, even the contemporary chronicler Roger of Wendover admits that this was just a rumor, and there is no concrete evidence for Langton's involvement.

Even though King John issued his own charter on the day of his coronation, promising that his duty was to provide and secure liberty and safety for all the people of England, the barons did not trust him. For this reason, they chose to invoke Henry's Coronation Charter. Furthermore, the older charter was more promising than John's. It detailed topics such as inheritance, marriage, wardship, and more—all points over which the barons had argued with the king. John's charter was eloquent and used vague words, but the barons wanted practical solutions to the problems they were facing, not distant promises of a better future. The barons were aware that

Henry's charter needed reworking to appeal to their troubles and their times, but it served as a good foundation for the reconstruction of the law and government.

On January 6, 1215, King John traveled to London to meet with the rebellious barons. The day was symbolic, as it was the last day of Christmas when, in old English tradition, kingship was celebrated. John wore the crown and expected his subjects to respect the symbolism of the day. However, the barons came armed and prepared, allowing no chance for the king to sway them from their determined path. Already politically weak, John lost the initiative. The meeting took place in the new Temple in London, an English seat of power belonging to the order of the Knights Templar. The Temple was neutral territory bordering London in the north, but it wasn't part of the great city. The armed barons demanded that John confirm the charter of Henry I, but the king asked for a delay instead. The meeting was fruitless, and open war seemed a possibility in the near future.

The barons had the support of some of the bishops, as they swore to sustain the house of the Lord. They also promised to bring liberty to the church and to the whole realm. King John demanded that the barons swear fealty to him. He added a clause to the traditional oath of allegiance that asked his subjects to support him, not only against all men but also against the charter.

As the meeting in the new Temple reached a standstill, John and the barons agreed to delay and scheduled the next meeting to be held on April 26th. Both sides used this pause to make tactical decisions that would give them an advantage over the opposing side. To confirm his alliance with the pope, and to be certain he would receive support from the Vatican, John "took the cross." which means that he vowed to join the crusade. This vow secured his protection from the church on all matters, as the medieval ecclesiastical law dictated. Pope Innocent III took the opportunity to officially condemn the actions of the rebellious barons. He also ordered them to put down arms and swear an oath to the king, threatening excommunication for anyone who refused to do so. The Pope also wrote to Langton, accusing him of failing to act as a mediator and bring peace to the kingdom. Once again, he ordered Langton to persuade the two sides to agree with each other at all costs.

As the day of the next meeting with the king approached, the barons gathered their armed forces at Stamford. They started their march towards Northampton, the location where the meeting was to take place. On route, they were joined by Robert Fitzwalter and Geoffrey Mandeville, Earl of Essex, accompanied by their own forces. The barons' army grew as they approached Northampton, becoming a substantial force that threatened the king. John, however, broke his word yet again. He did not come to the appointed meeting. Instead, he promised safe passage to anyone who would come to him to talk through the mediation of Archbishop Langton. The barons continued their march and met with Langton at Brackley, a manor belonging to the Earl of Winchester. There the barons drew up a list of demands they had for the king and presented it to Langton. This list would serve as the basis for the Magna Carta, and Langton made sure John would receive it. Upon hearing the demands, John immediately denounced them, saying that the barons were vain and unreasonable. He also said that if he granted them all the liberties they ask for, it would mean the king would become their slave, not their ruler.

The barons were given no other choice but to carry out their threat of civil war. They renounced their oaths of allegiance to the king on May 5th. Robert Fitzwalter became the commander-in-chief of the rebellion, and he took the title Marshal of the Army of God and the Holy Church in pure defiance of John's taking on the cross and his alliance with the Vatican. Their first goal was to lay siege to the castle at Northampton, the king's own property. There, the rebels faced their first losses. Many died in the fruitless siege, as they did not have any siege engines. Not wanting to lose even more people, the barons decided to give up on the Northampton Castle and instead continue their march to Bedford.

On May 9th, John issued a charter referring to all the demands of the rebelling barons. He promised the pope would act as chairman of the new commission made of eight barons, four of whom would be chosen from those who remained loyal to the king, and four of whom would be chosen by the rebels from amongst their own ranks. On May 10th, he promised free passage to the rebel barons without repercussions. Furthermore, he promised he would not arrest or attack the barons. However, only two days later, John issued an order allowing his men to seize the lands owned by the rebelling barons.

Using the opportunity of May 9th and John's charter, by which he promised to deal with all the demands of the rebels, the barons drew up a document that historians refer to as the "Unknown Charter of Liberties." Once again, the new charter was built on Henry's Charter of Liberties—using seven clauses directly from it—with new ones that had the purpose of reinforcing those existing liberties. King John tried to buy more time hoping that Pope Innocent III would back him up. However, the rebel barons did not find his delays appropriate. They could not lose momentum, so they decided to gather an army and attack London. In reply, John tried to gain the support of the citizens of London by issuing a special charter that would grant them certain rights and the ability to elect a new mayor every year. But Robert Fitzwalter had his own ties to London. As the lord of Baynard's Castle, he acted as the procurator of the city, a standard-bearer, and the commander of the city militia. Other than these official titles, he also had trade ties in London which granted him access to all classes of the population. Using his web of contacts and favors, Fitzwalter managed to secure the support of London's citizens for the rebelling barons. When the army arrived in London on May 17th, the gates of the city were open for them, and they took control of the city without any resistance.

Even though London was practically granted to them, Fitzwalter and the other barons decided to attack the Jews, demolish their houses, and use the materials to reinforce the city walls. The barons who continued to support the king were not spared, either. Their property was plundered and used to finance the cause, and their houses were burned down, demolished, or repurposed. The fall of the capital city was decisive. Many barons who were loyalists decided to join the rebellion–some out of fear for their lives and properties, others realizing where the political power lay. Only a few barons chose to resist, and they had to flee the city to continue supporting the king.

John was forced to agree on a truce, and he sent out his men to act as intermediaries on May 27th. He took up residence in Windsor Castle, where he remained during the negotiations. With the king in Windsor and the rebelling barons in Staines on The River Thames, there was only one place that was convenient for the meeting between the two conflicting parties: Runnymede. This place was a meadow on the south bank of the Thames, situated midway from Windsor and Staines. Because both parties came with armed forces behind them, any meeting place could easily become a battlefield. Runnymede was chosen because the ground was too wet and boggy; therefore, nobody would be mad enough to start a battle there.

Accompanied by Stephen Langton, King John came in person to meet the barons at Runnymede on July 10th. This was the date he set his seal on the peace treaty that contained all the terms the barons demanded. This document historians call the Articles of the Barons, as it is titled: "These are the Articles which the barons seek and which the king agrees."[1] Over the course of the next ten days,

---

[1] The Article of the Barons. (2014, September 15). Retrieved from https://www.bl.uk/collection-items/the-articles-of-the-barons

Stephen Langton managed to convert the articles into a charter. As an extraordinary peace mediator, Langton had to fulfill the demands of the barons and turn them into a peace proposal. When King John finally accepted the proposed treaty, he placed his seal on it as a symbol of agreement. The seal was the standard double-sided great seal of England, and it was attached to the document at the bottom using cords.

The seal of the Angevin dynasty was a reference to the Old Testament text in which the Jews demand to have a king: "...that our king may judge us, and go out before us and fight our battles."[2] On one side of the royal seal was a visual representation of a king as a judge, and on the other side was the image of a king as a military commander. It is ironic that John, a king who failed his nation in both instances–as a judge and as a battle commander–used this seal. History remembers him only as an unjust judge and an unsuccessful military leader who lost all of England's continental territories. Furthermore, the seal was now being used to surrender royal power rather than to enhance it, as it had in the past.

The document which was sealed at Runnymede was indeed The Great Charter, or Magna Carta. but it wouldn't be called by that name for a few more years. No matter what name was used at the time, the document was a symbol of the fast-changing politics of the 13th century and indicated the decline of royal power. Unlike the "Unknown Charter," which had only twelve articles, the Articles of the Barons had forty-eight. Amongst them was an article that granted liberties to the city of London, such as the freedom of trade and transportation on River Thames. The citizens of London did well by siding with the barons since their decision brought nothing but advantages to the city.

Even though Robert Fitzwalter took the title "Marshal of the Army of God and Holy Church," it is rather unusual that the

---

[2] Bible, Samuel 8,20

Articles of the Barons do not contain a single article that refers to the rights of the church. It is clear that the Articles tried to exclude the pope from English politics, and it is rather strange that King John agreed. The last article indeed says that the king has no right to ask the pope to revoke or diminish this document in any way. And even if he would try to do so, the document is secured, as no agreement of such nature between the king and the pope would be recognized by the law.

The distrust that the barons displayed for the king continued as they insisted on taking the Articles to London themselves. In fact, some of the barons did not find it satisfactory enough that the document was sealed by the king. They wanted even more proof of the king's goodwill. Therefore, Stephen Langton and other bishops of England, together with the papal legate Pandulf, were responsible for the king's behavior. They were tasked with securing the king's respect for the articles.

On June 15th, another plenary session was held at Runnymede. This date is celebrated in England as a historically important day when the Magna Carta was signed. The event is represented in English culture by various sculptors, painters, and writers. Politicians throughout history have used this event for their campaigns. Many tried to install the date as another bank holiday, a national public holiday in the United Kingdom. Even though the popular opinion is that the Magna Carta was signed on June 15th, there is no evidence to confirm this claim. Except for one contemporary writer's mention that a meeting was held at Runnymede on this date, there is no evidence to confirm what this meeting was about. It could not have been the signing for plenty of reasons: King John could not write, and in Medieval England, documents were acknowledged with a seal, not a manual signature. It is already known that the king sealed the Articles on June 10th. However, in medieval times, rulers would not stoop so low as to seal their own documents. For this purpose, there was a selected member of the Court of Chancery called a spigurnel, whose duty was to seal documents with the king's approval. History can only guess what happened on this date and if June 15th is the right date, as only one unknown writer mentions it.

It is generally believed that the concluding clause, numbered sixty-three, was added during the meeting on June 15th. This clause calls for the liberation of the church and reminds of the liberties and rights of citizens and their heirs:

"Wherefore we wish and firmly enjoin that the English church shall be free,

and that the men in our kingdom shall have and hold all the aforesaid

liberties, rights and concessions well and peacefully, freely and quietly,

fully and completely, for themselves and their heirs from us and our heirs,

in all matters and in all places for ever, as is aforesaid. An oath, moreover,

has been taken, as well on our part as on the part of barons, that all these

things aforesaid shall be observed in good faith and without evil

dispositions."[3]

This section from the Magna Carta can be treated as a clue to what happened on June 15th. It wasn't the signing of the Great Charter, as it is commonly believed, but rather the proclamation, conclusion, and promise of an oath.

The satisfied barons renewed their oaths of allegiance to the king four days later, on June 19th. The ceremony was rich, and the king wore the regalia of his grandmother, Empress Matilda. With the

---

[3] Magna Carta, Clause 63

Great Charter to ensure their rights, the barons were eager to swear fealty to their king. Contemporary writers agree there was no sign of animosity between the once-angry barons and King John during the oath-renewing ceremony, which took place at Runnymede.

In the period between June 10th and June 15th, even more articles were added to the Charter. Especially important is Clause 14, which describes the "common council" of the kingdom. The vague phrase "common council" was neatly defined as a summoned parliament-like assembly of barons, bishops, and major landlords who were now given the power to decide if new taxes were valid, justified, and of a reasonable amount.

# Chapter 3 – The Magna Carta

The 1215 Magna Carta written in Medieval Latin

(Source:https://en.wikipedia.org/wiki/Magna_Carta#/media/File:Magna_Carta_(British_Library_Cotton_MS_Augustus_II.106).jpg)

The Magna Carta was written in Latin and in prose. It was only later, in modern times, that it was divided into sixty-three clauses that appear to be a collection of statements that follow each other without any obvious order. However, when it is read in prose, it becomes an obvious critique of the rule of the Plantagenets, particularly John. The Magna Carta deals with political, legal, economic, ecclesiastical, and feudal matters—all of which were of great importance then and remain of great importance today, as well.

The document begins with a preamble, or introduction, in which King John addresses all the men of his kingdom. He retains, in this document, the titles Duke of Normandy, Duke of Aquitaine, and Count of Anjou, even though he lost those territories much earlier during his reign. The men he is addressing are listed as archbishops, bishops, abbots, barons, and earls, but he also names his servants: foresters, justices, sheriffs, reeves, and others. The most important part of the address is that it finishes with *omnibus fidelibus suis*, which translates to "all the faithful ones." By this, John made it known that the Great Charter was not granted to those who were not his loyal subjects. The Charter wasn't given freely, from the king to the people. It was valid only for those who would renew their oaths and swear fealty to the king. Only those who were faithful to the Crown had the right to enjoy the freedoms and peace guaranteed by the Magna Carta.

The document continues with a list of the king's advisors. There are twenty-seven names of people who worked on the Magna Carta. Most of them were bishops and barons who remained loyal to the king during the barons' revolt. These same names are repeated in Clause 62, where they are listed as witnesses to the document. As the prime mediator of the Magna Carta at Runnymede and even before, Stephen Langton is at the top of the list. He is described as "Primate of all England and Cardinal of the Holy Roman Church." No doubt, under his influence, the first clause of the Magna Carta deals with the status of the church.

The first words of the first clause in the Magna Carta are as follows: "Firstly, we have granted to God and confirmed by this, our present charter, for us and our heirs in perpetuity, that the English Church shall be free."[4]

It is commonly believed that this was Langton's attempt to, once and for all, deal with the issue that raged between the Plantagenet kings and the church since the 1160s when Henry II clashed with Thomas Becket. This first line that regards the church and its status is an echo of the opening remarks of Henry I's Coronation Charter, which had a prime influence on the Magna Carta. Langton managed to secure the fact that the king had no right to interfere in church elections. Perhaps his personal experience, when John refused to recognize him as Archbishop of Canterbury, gave him the motivation to fight for this cause specifically. Aside from being the first clause, there is another important aspect of this clause that describes the church and its liberties. After this clause ends, the king re-introduces the Great Charter with the following statement: "We have also granted to all the freemen of our realm ..." [5]This new start gives special importance to the clause that refers to the church. It is not only the first promise but also a separate promise to the church. As such, it is placed above all other promises the king made in the Magna Carta, which lead some historians to believe that the church enjoyed special protection.

The barons did not include the church in their articles when they first proposed such a document. However, the Magna Carta does refer to the English church. In fact, it placed the church above all else. Even though Langton came late to the negotiations, he managed to lift his own political interests to the top. As if to affirm the special status the church was given in this document, Clause 63

---

[4] Magna Carta Translation, Clause 1. (n.d.). Retrieved from https://www.archives.gov/exhibits/featured-documents/magna-carta/translation.html

[5] Magna Carta Translation, re-introduction. (n.d.). Retrieved from https://www.archives.gov/exhibits/featured-documents/magna-carta/translation.html

states the following: "We wish and firmly command that the English church shall be free and that men in our kingdom have and hold all the aforesaid liberties." [6]While the first draft of the Magna Carta in the form of the Barons' Articles was a secular document, the Magna Carta is not. In it, religious considerations take precedence and are treated separately from the rest of the document.

The next issue the Magna Carta dealt with was the most important one for the barons: the rights and reliefs of inheritance. In the second article, John promised that he would limit the royal inheritance fee to £100, and it would be equal for all earls, barons, and other great men of importance. The fee was lowered to 100 marks in the case of knights. As a side note, the mark in Medieval England wasn't a coin but a unit of accounting introduced by the Danes. One mark was worth thirteen shillings and fourpence.

Consequently, the king would not charge outrageous amounts of money for the right to inherit lands and properties. Cases such as that of William FitzAlan, who was charged £10,000 to receive his inheritance, would not repeat. Through other clauses, the king promised he would not force his men into bankruptcy to retain political control over them. He would not seize land or other properties for a debt if the debtor could repay with his personal possessions. The process of determining the wealth of a deceased person was given in detail. Exchequers had no right to extort, bully, and ruin people, and they were placed under strict supervision (Clause 26 and 27).

Other clauses of the Magna Carta referred to various aspects of the law of inheritance. Widows did not pay the inheritance fee to the king and were given access to their portion of the property immediately after the death of their husbands. Clauses 7 and 8 also made sure widows would not be married again against their will.

---

[6] Magna Carta Translation, Clause 63. (n.d.). Retrieved from https://www.archives.gov/exhibits/featured-documents/magna-carta/translation.html

However, this does not mean that the Magna Carta was liberal when it came to the rights of women. For example, Clause 54 states: "No man shall be arrested or imprisoned because of the appeal of a woman for the death of anyone but her husband." [7]

Clause 3 states that young men who were not yet of the legal age of maturity would not be forced to pay the king's fee for an inheritance but would be able to inherit their possessions only when they reached the legal age of adulthood. Under Clause 37, young men were protected from the king's will to seize them and claim them as his wards. Anyone who was granted the wardship of minors was to be respectful of his inheritance and not use it for personal gain.

Clauses 10 and 11 of the Magna Carta dealt with debts to Jewish moneylenders and to the king, who was forbidden from pursuing high-interest loans through his own officials. Clause 13 confirms London's ancient liberties, as it was the city that played a key role in the negotiations between the king and the revolting barons. The merchants who inhabited London were given freedom of movement, both on land and on water. They were also exempted from the "evil tolls." The same clause then describes how foreign merchants should be treated during times of war.

People seeking justice now had the Court of Common Pleas, which had a fixed location. Until the Magna Carta, the citizens of the kingdom had to find John and ask for an audience. Magna Carta guaranteed county courts would be held at a fixed time and at a fixed place throughout the year, and the fines for offenses were to be within reasonable amounts (Clauses 17-22).

Clause 35 of the Magna Carta regulated measures for all the important things in the kingdom, such as corn, cloth, ale, and grain.

---

[7] Magna Carta Translation, Clause 54. (n.d.). Retrieved from https://www.archives.gov/exhibits/featured-documents/magna-carta/translation.html

Purveyance was banned by the document, which meant that royal officials could no longer confiscate goods, grain, or horses for the king's personal use. If the king was in immediate need of such things, his officials had to pay for them.

Clause 44 concerned the people who lived outside the forest lands and protected them from being judged by forest law. Clauses 47 and 48 touched on the forest law, as well, limiting the boundaries of the forest and urging the investigation of corruption among forest officials.

The Magna Carta dealt with common law but also with grand ideas. It is no wonder some of its clauses were used for over eight centuries. For example, Clause 21 states that barons and earls could be fined only by their peers and "in accordance with the offense."[8] Another clause that was long-lived is Clause 45. It says: "Judges, sheriffs, and other royal officials are to be competent." Later, Clause 39 was expanded and became one of the most enduring and relevant statements of any constitutional document. Its final shape is as follows:

"No free man is to be arrested, or imprisoned or disseized, or outlawed, or exiled, or in any other way ruined, nor will we go or send against him, except by the legal judgment of his peers or by the law of the land (*nisi per legale judicium parum sourum*)."[9]

There is no doubt that this clause was designed with the intention of stopping King John from legally pursuing some of his greatest men. Together with Clause 40, which simply says, "To no one will we sell, to no one will we deny or delay, right or justice," Clause 39 is the foundation of the principles of trial by jury. It also carries the

---

[8] Magna Carta Translation, Clause 21. (n.d.). Retrieved from https://www.archives.gov/exhibits/featured-documents/magna-carta/translation.html

[9] Magna Carta Translation, Clause 39. (n.d.). Retrieved from https://www.archives.gov/exhibits/featured-documents/magna-carta/translation.html

basic idea that justice should always restrain the government from abusing its power.

The Magna Carta is a far-reaching document, yet much of it remains vague, and some areas of the Magna Carta seem unfinished. Some clauses were clearly intended to push some of the complex political issues of the time; however, they feel rushed or abandoned mid-sentence. For example, Clauses 49, 50, and 51 speak of the king's promise to release all hostages and give charters to the people of England as security of peace. He also promised he would expel foreign knights and mercenary soldiers; however, there are no details as to when and where this would happen. These clauses seem like the beginning of an idea, but much is left unspoken.

Clauses 39 and 40 are, to this day, considered the foundations of modern Western democracy, but Clause 61 is of equal importance. It is known as the "security clause" by which men who lived in 1215 found a way to hold the king to his word given in the Great Charter. Without it, the king was free to break his promises to the people and return to his old ways of rule. The security clause speaks of a possible scenario where, if the king was to "transgress against any of the articles of the peace ...", a council of twenty-five barons was under the full right to "distrain upon and distress us in all ways possible, by taking castles, lands and possessions and in any other ways they can ... saving our person and the persons of our queen and children." [10]This meant that if the king broke his promises, he would have to face the wrath of his own subjects. The Magna Carta made civil war legal, which is rather strange for a document that was to ensure peace.

There are only four parchment versions of the Magna Carta that survive to this day. Two of them are held in the British Library (of

---

[10] Magna Carta Translation, Clause 61. (n.d.). Retrieved from https://www.archives.gov/exhibits/featured-documents/magna-carta/translation.html

which one is badly damaged by a fire that occurred in 1731), the third is secured in the Salisbury Cathedral, and the fourth is kept in Lincoln Castle. There are variations among these four documents, but they are all replicas of the agreement. They all bear a stamp of authenticity, a double-sided wax royal seal attached to the bottom of the documents with a short silk cord. There were many more copies of the Magna Carta, and many copies and reissues survived in archives around the world, but only these four documents are considered the "original" charters. It is unknown if there was ever one original document from which all the copies were made or if the copies were made simultaneously. The signing of the Magna Carta is often depicted romantically, with the king ceremonially signing the document, but as discussed above, that probably never happened. Many of the events that surround the creation of the Magna Carta remain a mystery. History can only guess how the process of turning a peace agreement into a document with constitutional principles took place, and it took a long time to finish.

# Chapter 4 – The Failure of the Magna Carta

History often places the blame for the failure of the Magna Carta solely on King John. Although he is not without blame, the barons weren't saints either. They quickly started abusing their newly gained power, similarly to John at his worst. The barons were aware that John would try to wiggle out of the Great Charter, considering his systematic dishonesty in the past. The barons were determined to stop him. The already mentioned Clause 61 gave the barons the much-needed liberty to act if the king was breaking his promises. This clause was solely the work of the barons, as it came directly from the Articles of the Barons, and was not changed by the royal clerks, as other articles were. The barons did not trust anyone, and they took it upon themselves to write Clause 61 in detail and in full so that it wouldn't be tampered with. The article was written in a long paragraph of continuous prose.

Clause 61 begins this way: "This is the *forma securitatis* [formula, or terms of security] for the preservation of the peace and liberties between the king and the kingdom." [11]As mentioned in the previous chapter, this clause sets up the council, or panel, of twenty-five

[11] Magna Carta Translation, Clause 61. (n.d.). Retrieved from https://www.archives.gov/exhibits/featured-documents/magna-carta/translation.html

barons, chosen by the baronage. The council had far-reaching powers that were to be used to "... observe, maintain and cause to be observed the peace and liberties which we have granted."[12] If the articles of the Great Charter were not respected by the king or his officials, the four barons of the council were to be informed. These four had the power to conduct their own investigation, which would confirm a possible breach of the Charter. If the breach was not rectified within forty days of its committing, the four barons would be obliged to notify the council of twenty-five. The council was then to punish the king until, in their own judgment, the king made amends. The *forma securitatis* promised the barons great power, which was to be used to limit the king. Nothing was off-limits to the barons except hurting the king, queen, and their children.

Every citizen had to obey and assist the twenty-five in their judgment and actions. Some barons were even empowered to act on behalf of the whole council, as they had the role of overruling the absent or dissenter barons. The twenty-five were meant to represent public safety. They were a self-recruited and permanent committee, which probably had the intention of becoming an aristocratic oligarchy if given enough time. If allowed, they would turn England into something like the Republic of Venice, where the king was just a puppet to his aristocratic rulers. However, the twenty-five never lived long enough as a political entity to reach their goals. Still, they had an immediate role to play.

As soon as the Magna Carta was ratified, the council of barons took it upon themselves to correct all the king's wrongs. They had among their ranks many of the barons who were casualties of King John's rule. They were to judge each separate case and demand compensation. Furthermore, they had the right to assert the extent of the compensation the king had to pay—be it with money, lands

---

[12] Magna Carta Translation, Clause 61. (n.d.). Retrieved from https://www.archives.gov/exhibits/featured-documents/magna-carta/translation.html

and castles, or other possessions. The twenty-five went so far as to use their newfound power to humiliate John, their former oppressor. Clause 61, the famous *forma securitatis*, clearly states that the four who were to represent and investigate the case should "come to Us," meaning they were supposed to go to the king to state their case. However, the barons considered this task beneath their dignity, so they demanded that the king come to them. In fact, while King John was sick with gout and in bed, they refused to come to his chambers or even excuse the king's presence. King John had to be carried on a litter in front of the twenty-five, who then proceeded to judge him. The barons were intentionally showing off their power. It was a calculated move since King John had to comply. He was in a rush to conclude the cases, and fifty of the disputes were solved within the next ten days. During this time, twelve of the twenty-five panel members benefited greatly from the settled disputes. For instance, Richard de Clare received Buckingham, Robert Fitzwalter was given Hertford Castle, and Henry de Bohun came into possession of the manors of the honour of Trowbridge. However, King John did not simply agree with all the terms the barons placed in front of him. He occasionally protested and would not give in. But the barons would place him under such pressure that, by the end of the day, he would simply have to give in.

John was extremely weak after the Runnymede events. He lacked the respect of his subjects and had little to no power. On top of it all, he lost his capital city, London. The barons simply refused to give the city of London back to the king, even though they promised during the meeting at Runnymede to do so if the king would fulfill certain obligations. The Magna Carta itself did not deal with the issue of London. There is a separate document that records the agreement between the king and the barons on how to deal with the city. The document was titled "Convention," and it stated that if the king fulfilled special conditions, London would be given back to him on August 15, 1215. Until then, it was under the custody of Robert Fitzwalter and the panel of twenty-five barons. If the king failed to deliver his end of the deal, the city would remain in the custody of the barons. This agreement was written twice, and each party received their own copy. Only the copy that was in the king's possession survived and is kept in The National Archives. What is truly remarkable about this document is that it treats London as private property, and it also treats the king as a private person rather than the sovereign of a nation.

The terms of this document, classified as "indenture" were spelled out quite clearly. Local commissions of twelve knights were to investigate the local sheriffs and other royal officials and search for proof of violations of the forest law. The king's obligation was to meet all the claims against him and restore all the rights and properties of damaged individuals. The indenture gave only a two months' timeframe for this endeavor to be achieved. John had no other choice but to comply. After all, by doing what he was told, he could only gain back the trust of the English people, who might even give him their support once more. After the uprising and small civil war that happened before Runnymede, the population of England mostly stayed neutral. The king's loyalists were a minority, but the followers of the rebellious barons were a minority, too.

The political struggle to gain the favor of a large, neutral population began. While John started accepting his part of the promise, the barons organized tournaments and celebrations to entertain their army and gain even more followers. However, John did only half of what he was supposed to do and started claiming he won't do anything else unless the barons would give him something in return. He complained he was the only one working actively on peace while the barons did nothing. He asked them to make charters that would confirm their allegiance, but the barons refused to do so. Their refusal was exactly what the king hoped for, as it would give him political advantage. He was then able to create a picture of a benevolent king who was doing everything within his power to keep the peace, while the barons refused to keep their end of the deal.

The next meeting between King John and the barons was scheduled in Oxford on August 15th, a day after the expiration of the deadline given by the London indenture. The king did not show up in person. Instead, he sent a delegation to convey his message. They were instructed to say how the king had surrendered many things, as agreed, but had received nothing in return. The king continued to accuse the barons of causing him personal harm. He even went so far as to proclaim that he was afraid for his own life since the barons had gathered a large army. Smart enough, he did not call for the breakup of the Runnymede deal. He was simply complaining that the settlement achieved two months ago was not going forward as planned.

In return, the barons agreed to have yet another meeting with the king by the end of August. However, that meeting never happened, as it was right then when the barons learned that King John had already asked Rome to annul the Magna Carta. In fact, he had sent letters to Pope Innocent III back in May, on the very eve after the Runnymede meeting, complaining of the barons' behavior. By June 22nd, he sent another letter that asked Innocent III to annul the Great Charter. But in medieval times, it took months for letters to reach their destination, especially when traveling as far as Rome. The pope did not receive the news from England until November of 1215, and he was completely oblivious of the summer events between John and the barons.

Earlier that year, Innocent III had sent three letters to all involved parties in the English dispute: King John, the barons, and Langton–who, as you may remember, acted as a mediator and was supposed to resolve the conflict. His letters were written in the form of a sovereign addressing his subjects. Naturally, he expected Langton to do exactly as he was told, and the barons were expected to obey. Under the threat of excommunication, the barons were ordered to stop any violent treachery towards John and to regard the king with all the royal honors his title bore. When the pope received word from John that the barons had not listened to his instructions, he was furious. The barons had openly defied the pope, and Langton had not proceeded to excommunicate them. The Pope felt an obligation to teach them a lesson on obedience.

As a response, Innocent III issued a papal edict titled "*Mirari cogimur et moveri*" (We are compelled to wonder and be moved). In this bull (a type of public decree), the pope proclaimed King John to be innocent and a good Christian obedient to the church. Further, he mentioned Langton's failure to protect the king and accused him of conspiring with the rebellious barons. The Pope also accused the barons, whom he called "worse than Saracens,"[13] of trying to get rid of John and–by their actions–of preventing John from joining the holy war. Pope Innocent III took this opportunity to excommunicate the barons as well as their accomplices. He ordered the bishops and archbishops to proclaim the sentence of excommunication throughout England. He even threatened them with suspension if they decided to disobey.

Langton was stunned by the pope's letter. He saw himself as nothing more than a mediator who had tried to resolve the dispute between the king and the barons. However, the pope instructed him to abandon his neutrality and the role of a mediator. He was to openly take the king's side in the dispute. Langton had no choice, and he proceeded to obey the pope's orders. At the conference at Staines, in August, Langton excommunicated all who disturbed the peace in the kingdom, keeping the ceremony vague. He was not prepared to take the king's side, and he did not want to give up his neutrality. He also didn't want to excommunicate each one of the barons by name. Instead, the task fell to three commissioners whom

[13] *Selected Letters of Pope Innocent III concerning England (1198-1216)*, ed. C.R. Cheney and W. H. Semple (London, 1953) 196-7 no.75, from the dorse of the Patent Roll (*Mirari cogimur et moveri*, 19 March 1215).

the pope had already prepared in case Langton failed to do as instructed. They were Bishop of Winchester Peter des Roches, papal legate Pandulf, and the Abbot of Reading. On September 5th, the three published a letter specifying each baron's name and the deed for which they were being excommunicated. They also placed London under an interdict because the city had openly supported the barons during the civil war. Some of the clerical associates of the punished barons were also excommunicated, such as the Bishop of Hereford and the Archdeacon of Hereford.

Langton had been at the political center of English life ever since he was appointed to the position of Archbishop of Canterbury, and the Magna Carta crisis emphasized his role in politics. However, his failure to obey the pope's orders marked the immediate end of his political career. His refusal to name the barons who were excommunicated led to his suspension, as the pope had promised would happen to all who disobeyed.

In September, the Bishop of Winchester imposed Langton's penalty. In vain, Langton appealed to Rome. The pope only confirmed his suspension, deciding Langton should end his political and religious career in humiliation. Langton had to leave England, and at the same time as his departure, another letter from Pope Innocent arrived. In this letter, the pope denounced the Magna Carta, declared it dishonorable and shameful. He ordered John to break his oath to the Magna Carta by proclaiming it annulled and invalid. The Magna Carta was dead, and it achieved nothing for the short life it had. What followed was a civil war known as the First Barons' War.

# Chapter 5 – The War

The Magna Carta was an ambitious peacemaking document, but it was also a great failure. The Great Charter failed to bind the king to his promises, and it failed to reconcile John to the northerners. Pope Innocent III annulled the document within months of its declaration, an act that brought back civil war and times of anarchy. In time, the Magna Carta would become one of the most revered documents in English history, but 1215 was not the year it happened.

It is unknown whether King John ever intended to stick to the terms presented in the Magna Carta. By July, he had probably abandoned such an idea, as he wrote to Pope Innocent III requesting the annulment of the document. In his letter, he claimed that the terms for the Magna Carta were extracted from him with threats of violence and, as such, were not binding. The pope was happy to agree, and by September 1215, he sent letters to England in which he expressed anger that John, a papal vassal, was treated so by his subjects. As John's superior, he had all the right to release the king from the obligations which the Magna Carta imposed on him. The English translation of Pope Innocent III's letter was printed in *English Historical Documents*, and it says the following: "Although our well-beloved son in Christ, John illustrious King of the English, grievously offended God and the Church ... the king at length returned to his senses ... But the enemy of the human race [Satan] who always hates good impulses, by his cunning wiles, stirred up against him the barons of England so that, with a wicked inconstancy, the men who supported him when injuring the Church rebelled against him when he turned from his sin. ..." The pope took a firm tone right from the beginning of his letters. Innocent III accused the barons of being unreasonable, treacherous, and aggressive. He accused the whole English nation of shameful actions that thwarted the plans for the crusade in the holy land. The pope finished his letters by stating: "We utterly reject and condemn this settlement and under threat of excommunication we order that the king should not dare to observe it and that the barons and their associates should not require it to be observed."[14] With these words, Pope Innocent III annulled the Magna Carta. He excommunicated nine barons and all the citizens of London who he openly blamed for the duress that King John had to endure.

The result of the Magna Carta's annulment was the resumption of civil war. It was clear to the barons that King John would not be reformed or controlled in any way. John's behavior turned out to be quite contrary to the barons' wishes. By September 17th, John returned to his habit of seizing baronial estates by force. It was no wonder his opponents started resisting his rule once again. They ignored royal officials and even went so far as to replace them with their own barons' men. They refused to pay the money owed to the Crown. The most drastic action John's opposition undertook was the development of plans to replace the king. John threatened Archbishop Langton, who refused to give up his Rochester Castle. The argument ended up with the siege of the castle, which had a vital strategical position. At the same time, this siege was also the first armed conflict that started the First Barons' War.

Rochester Castle sits on the Roman road known as Watling Street. This road was a lifeline for Britain. Armies used it to easily transport men, mercenaries, arms, and supplies from the

---

[14] English Historical Documents, Vol. III, op.cit., pp.324-6

continental territories to Dover, and then move them all over England. Rochester Castle was granted to the Archbishops of Canterbury by Henry I. This is how it, eventually, went into Langton's hands. John reached an agreement with the Archbishop that the castle would be returned to the royal house once the Magna Carta was signed, but Langton refused to give up the castle, trying to remain neutral in the conflict to the very end. At the end of September of 1215, when Langton had already left England, the castle was finally surrendered to the barons.

John occupied the castle on October 13$^{th}$ as a response to the barons who decided to station a garrison in Rochester. John's army was larger, and the barons never came to help defend their castle. The defenders at Rochester Castle managed to resist for five weeks before they were forced to surrender due to supply exhaustion.

The barons were bold enough to write letters to Louis the Lion, a French prince and son of Philip Augustus. They invited him to join their cause, invade England, and take the crown for himself. The northern barons invited Alexander II of the Scots to invade Northumbria, Westmorland, and Cumberland. In Wales, Llywelyn ap Iorwerth (Llywelyn the Great) proclaimed himself a prince and captured all English-held castles in his territory. By December, a party of French knights arrived in London. John had to divide his attention to face possible attacks from three foreign princes as well as his subjects.

John finally began to feel the pressure the barons were putting on his hold of England, and his power began to weaken. He decided the north caused the most trouble, and he went to deal with the situation in the borderlands. The town of Berwick was the first to fall to John in the first days of 1216. To show off his power, John decided to burn the town, hoping it would be enough to scare off his enemies. His whole campaign in the north was designed to intimidate and bring terror to his subjects. He wanted to make sure they would realize he was still a king and had all the power over them. He continued to destroy and burn villages and farms. He allowed his soldiers, who were mostly mercenaries, to rape, murder, and steal. John also forced men to pay money for their and their families' freedom, as he was in constant need of money to finance his army.

The campaign against the Scots in the north was a success, and King John now turned toward the southeast. He brutalized Lincoln and Fotheringay on his way to East Anglia and Essex before turning west toward Oxford. He made the defeated rebels swear an oath to renounce the Magna Carta. People were afraid of his army, and resistance started to weaken. Some barons decided to turn their castles over to John without resistance just at the sight of his army. By March 1216, the barons started considering peace with John and probably would have given in if a rumor about Louis preparing to set sail for England had not started to circulate in April. Even John started preparing for a French invasion, fortifying the coast around Kent and sending his fleet across the Channel. The fleet's task was to try to block Louis in port and prevent him from even setting sail. However, they were unsuccessful, and the French prince landed in England at the end of May. At the sight of French sails, John decided to retreat to Winchester. Louis led his army through Kent toward London, where he was greeted with much cheer on June 2nd. There, he made a promise to restore all the old English laws and rule as a just king, while Fitzwalter and Mayor William Handel led the rebels and the London citizens to pay homage to Louis and admit him as their sovereign. Only four days later, Louis took upon himself the task of pursuing John.

The French prince proved to be worthy of his nickname "Louis the Lion" due to not only his military successes but also his political prowess. He didn't bring just his army from France. He came with carefully prepared propaganda, the author of which was probably Simon Langton, brother to Stephen Langton and Louis' chancellor. It is well known that Simon joined Louis in his invasion of England, helping him craft his claim to the throne. He claimed a hereditary right to the realm of England because his wife was Blanche, daughter of Queen Eleanor of Castile, who was the sister of Richard the Lionheart. He also claimed John lost his right to the throne when he betrayed his brother Richard while he was fighting in the crusade.

The second part of Louis' propaganda claimed he was elected to be king of England. Here, Louis called on the Charter, by which allegiance to the king was not legally given; it was a contract between the people and the king–a contract King John broke the first time when he handed England to Pope Innocent III without the consent of the barons. The second time John broke this contract was when he refused to comply with the Magna Carta and returned to his misgovernment. Louis stated that, given the circumstances, the barons had no other choice but to offer the crown to him.

Interestingly, Louis never promised to bring back the Magna Carta, only the old laws of England. And the barons did not seem to care. They still gave him their full support. This might mean that the barons didn't care about the Magna Carta itself and that John and Innocent III were somewhat right to denounce it. What the barons cared about most was their power, and it was of little interest to them how they would gain that power–be it through the Magna Carta or through a puppet king, such as Louis seemed to agree to be. It also might be that the barons–especially Fitzwalter and his cousin de Quincy–were so desperate to get rid of John, they simply didn't bother to name the terms when they invited the French prince to take the English crown.

The barons who were previously loyal to John started defecting. Even the new papal legate, Guala Bicchieri, was unable to fortify John's cause. Among the defecting barons was John's half-brother William Longspée, Earl of Salisbury. John's army was weakened, and Louis managed to push him out of southeastern England. Encouraged by the events in England, the Scots attacked the borders once more and besieged some of the northern castles. Anarchy took over the country while the battle between the two kings, Louis of France and John of England, continued.

King John was powerless and decided to retreat to his favorite residence, Corfe Castle, while Louis was advancing through England undisturbed. The French prince besieged Winchester, a castle that managed to hold only for ten days. They sent word to John of their inability to resist the siege, and John permitted them to surrender. Winchester was considered the second capital of England, and it was shameful to surrender it without a fight. The second wave of defection followed. Disappointed by King John's cowardice, some of his loyalists abandoned him, joining forces with Louis. Over two-thirds of the loyal barons left the king and chose to either join the rebels or stay neutral and avoid the conflict. The barons weren't the only ones who changed sides. Two-thirds of John's knights left, as well as the royal administrators and some of his household.

Louis now held most of the country, while King John was left with only three castles to give resistance to the French invader: Dover, Lincoln, and Windsor. Soon, even these three castles were under siege. It was then that John decided to put up a resistance. He marched northeast toward his garrison in Lincoln, where he hoped to meet Alexander of the Scots and punish him for giving his allegiance to Louis. However, Alexander wasn't there, and John had to satisfy himself by burning and looting Cambridgeshire to punish East Anglia for giving support to the rebellious barons.

It seemed that the war would be long and merciless, as John expected help from his ally the Pope. However, in October of 1216, Pope Innocent III died. This was an event that influenced the war in England to its core. John was disappointed his protector and ally was suddenly out of the game. He could not rely on Rome's help anymore. On top of that, he received word that the Castle in Dover, his main stronghold in the battle against the French, could not endure the siege for much longer.

While staying in Norfolk, John fell ill with dysentery. The illness did not stop him from pushing his army forward, however. On October 12th, he urged his troops across the Wellstream River without thinking of the territory's conditions. The tide was not in far enough, and much of his army's rations, horses, and some men were swallowed by quicksand. Among the lost items were royal treasures, such as John's coronation regalia–items forever lost to history, never to be seen again.

John escaped the quicksand safely, but he was ill and furious. His illness was treated with ripe peaches and new cider which, by today's standards of medicine, could only worsen his symptoms. He pushed his court to continue traveling, but he was in such agony he had to be carried. The procession reached Newark, where John would die on October 18th. Before he died, he was persuaded to forgive his enemies. John had enough loyalists remaining by his side to fulfill his dying wish to bury him in Worcester, next to the shrine of St. Wulfstan.

# Chapter 6 – The Regent and the End of the First Barons' War

When King John died, his son and heir was only nine years old. To help him ascend to the throne in a war-torn country, John appointed a council of thirteen executors whose task was to guide King Henry III in his rule and help him regain his kingdom. A minor ascending the throne in the medieval world was often disastrous, as a child was an easy target to the political opponents of the current regime. Age was not the only problem Henry III had to face at the start of his rule. More than half of England was under foreign rule, which had the support of most of the aristocracy. Under such circumstances, it is amazing that Henry III defied all expectations and managed to not only claim the throne but also thrive as a ruler. Henry's accession saved the House of Anjou, the kingdom, and the Great Charter. But it wasn't the child-king who was to be thanked for it. Largely, Henry III owed everything he was and everything he possessed to the Earl of Pembroke, William Marshal, appointed by John himself to be Henry's guardian.

William Marshal, one of the most famous knights of England, was seventy years old when he took on the role of caretaker for young Henry III. Marshal was the younger son of a minor nobleman; therefore, he had no lands or fortune and had to fight his way through life. He began training as a knight in Normandy, at a court of his cousin, William de Tancarville. Contrary to popular belief, studying for knighthood involved learning Biblical history, Latin, and the politics of the courts. William was knighted in 1166 during the campaign in Normandy, which was invaded by Flanders. The very next year, he tried the tournament for the first time, and there he found his true calling. William Marshal was tall, handsome, and strong, and as such, he easily became a star in tournaments. His martial skills with the lance and sword brought him international fame, money, and a very wealthy wife later in life. It also opened the doors of the Angevine court to him. He was a part of Queen Eleanor's escort when she was ambushed. Although the queen managed to escape, young William was caught and taken as a prisoner. Hearing of his bravery, Queen Eleanor paid for his ransom and once more employed him in her service, from where he was later transferred to serve as a combat tutor to young Henry III. Together, the young king and Marshal traveled Europe joining various tournaments. Even though later William was accused of having an affair with the king's wife, the friendship between the two remained strong, and Henry would ask for William on his deathbed. After the death of the young king, William Marshal joined the crusade and traveled to Jerusalem, but nothing is known of his deeds there.

William was forty-three when he married the seventeen-year-old daughter of Richard de Clare, Earl of Pembroke. Marshal suddenly had a claim over the large estates in England, most notably Wales and Ireland, as well as in Normandy. This marriage transformed William from a landless knight and son of a minor noble to one of the richest men in England who would become the Earl of Pembroke after his father-in-law's death. During the reign of Richard, John's older brother, William was in the king's service and supported him during the war in Normandy against Philip II of France. When John became the king in 1199, William offered him his services and proved to be loyal to the Crown. Even though his relationship with John cooled of and even escalated to outright hostility at one point, William Marshal stayed loyal to King John during his initial conflict with the barons. During the meeting at Runnymede where the Magna Carta was signed, Marshal supported the king, and he stayed loyal through the First Barons' War. His name is often mentioned as the leading negotiator between the king and the barons. William is also listed as the first of the noblemen who advised the king concerning the Magna Carta at Runnymede. His loyalty to the Crown was probably most displayed when he took responsibility for the funeral of the much-hated King John.

Interestingly, John is the first English king who left a testament behind him. This document was hurried, and it contained only sixteen lines, as John was aware he had no time to deal with all his possessions. The testament mostly deals with the salvation of the king's soul. Churches were to receive donations to repair the injuries they had endured by the king's hand. He also rewarded his faithful servants and specified the distribution of alms for the poor. His testament also contained instructions on how and where to bury him. The rest was left to his administrators to deal with as they saw fit. In the end, the document contained the names of thirteen councilors who were to help his son restore the kingdom. Two prominent names stood out: Cardinal Guala Bicchieri was named leader of the churchmen whose names were on the list, and William Marshal was named leader of the nobles who were chosen as councilors.

William Marshal was named not only the protector of the boy-king Henry III but also the regent of England—or at least this is what history leads us to believe. The only source of this information is a biographer of William Marshal, who may have been biased due to the personal nature of the topic. Although some historians are eager to dispute that Marshal was named regent, it is a plausible event. He was already one of the richest men in the kingdom and had great influence in court and generally in politics. Besides, he was the pillar of John's regime. To secure the success of the dynasty, who would have been a better choice than the chivalrous knight William Marshal?

Marshal rushed Henry III's coronation, as the political scene of England was uncertain. He hoped to gain a foothold with the ceremony, so only ten days after John's death, on October 28th, Henry III was crowned at Gloucester. The very next day, the council of thirteen gathered, where Marshal begged to be excused from the role of regent, due to his advanced age. The second choice for a regent was Earl Ranulf de Blondeville, who raised objections to his qualifications and praised Marshal as the only suitable candidate. The new papal legate, Guala Bicchieri, promised William absolution from all his sins, and it seems this was the act that convinced the old Earl of Pembroke to accept the regency.

Guala was sent to England as the new papal legate of Innocent III, who died only a few months later. His role was to protect John and Rome's interests in England. With the new pope, Honorius III, and the new king of England, Henry III, the politics between these two sides did not change. The pope was still the overlord of England, and the young king had to pay him homage and acknowledge him as his superior. Guala was an enthusiastic enforcer of these politics, and his first act as papal legate was to excommunicate Prince Louis and his associates who helped him in the invasion of England. With William Marshal as regent, Guala was even more certain of his actions, and he went so far as to call for a crusade against Louis, uniting the church and the state into a common cause against the French.

On November 12, 1216, William Marshal and the council of thirteen advised the young King Henry III to reissue the Magna Carta. However, it was the Magna Carta transformed. First to suffer transformation was Clause 61, the famous *forma securitatis*. After all, it was the clause that went against everything the loyalists and the pope stood for. In it, the Great Charter was described as more important than an oath to a king. Furthermore, it gave immense power to the panel of twenty-five barons, who were supposed to act as bringers of justice and whose goal was to elevate the king into a role like that of the Venetian doge.

Next to be transformed was Clause 48, which commissioned twelve knights to investigate John's forest law. The problem the knights presented for the new king was their ability to transform into a powerful entity, like the panel of twenty-five but on a local level. The power they could gain posed a threat to the stability of the Crown. Clauses that required the king to compensate immediately for all the misgovernment of John's rule had to be removed. Others were labeled as important, but to be considered later. The core of the Great Charter was left intact. Feudal incidents were to be settled according to the Magna Carta, justice administration was to be reformed, weights and measures were to be standardized, and trade was given guaranteed freedom. The core of the Magna Carta became the new law, with improvements and clarifications in places that needed it.

Since all of John's regalia was kept in Winchester, which was still occupied by the enemies of the Crown, Henry III had no seals with which to declare the Great Charter. Instead, it was Guala who sealed the document as a representative of the pope, the king's superior. This meant that the pope himself endorsed the reissued Charter, even though Rome annulled it in its previous form. What changed so significantly that the pope suddenly accepted the Charter? It wasn't just its transformation to better suit the king. It was also a convenient thing to do since Louis himself failed to commit to the Magna Carta or to reissue it. The people also believed in the revised Charter, and the proof for that is the fact that William Marshal sent copies to Ireland, where the twenty-five had no power. Ireland stayed loyal to John in his struggles against the barons. The reissued Magna Carta was a proper basis on which to rebuild the royal government once Louis was dealt with. They also hoped the new Charter would appease the barons, who would once again swear fealty to the Crown.

The newly-transformed Magna Carta did not manage to bring back the barons. They did not offer their support to Henry, as William Marshal hoped they would. The king's opposition hardened. But Louis could not be officially crowned a king, even though Westminster Abbey was under his control. Henry was the one who had the support of the pope and the English church. Despite this, William Marshal had to deal with several months of political stalemate. War campaigns were usually suspended during the winter, and this one was no different. In February of 1217, Louis departed England in hopes of bringing reinforcements from France. While Louis was away, the barons were garrisoned in London once more. To pass the time while waiting for the French reinforcements, the barons decided to organize a tournament. However, the tournament gained a voice of its own, and the knights, barons, and army embarked on a journey through the English midlands to attempt to free Mountsorrel Castle in Leicestershire. This castle belonged to none other than Saer de Quincy, 1st Earl of Winchester and cousin to Robert Fitzwalter. It was also occupied by the royalists at the time of the tournament. Louis returned to England just in time to join the endeavor in Leicestershire, bringing the army from France. In total, there were around six hundred knights and one thousand footmen. Saer de Quincy personally led the English army joined by Fitzwalter, while the French troops were under the command of the Count of Perche.

The royalists who occupied the Mountsorrel Castle were no match for the army of rebels and the French prince. They had to withdraw to Nottingham to avoid the blood-spill, and Mountsorrel was freed simply by a display of force. Somewhat disappointed in the lack of resistance, the barons and soldiers searched for an opportunity, which presented itself not long after. Fifty miles northeast of Mountsorrel Castle lie Lincoln, with a castle that had resisted the rebels throughout the Barons' War. Lincoln Castle was besieged for a very long time, and when the rebels heard of the barons' forces being so near, they begged for help. Fitzwalter and de Quincy were eager to help their fellow rebels while Louis stayed in London. However, Nottingham was on their way to Lincoln. To avoid the royalist forces stationed there, the barons decided to turn east and cut their path through the agricultural lands of the Vale of Belvoir, where they looted and pillaged as they went. Taking this route, the baronial forces managed to approach Lincoln unchallenged and without any losses.

William Marshal was at Northampton when the news of the barons' army joining the besiegers at Lincoln arrived. He took the opportunity of Louis' forces being divided and tried to destroy them. He rode for four days from Northampton to Newark, but instead of going straight to Lincoln, he made a detour to the west, positioning himself to approach Lincoln from the northwest. If the rebels expected any help to come to the Lincoln royalists, they expected it to come from the southwest. He didn't just have the advantage of surprise on the battlefield; he also had access to the castle's west entrance, as it was not yet controlled by the rebels. The rebels didn't know about the existence of the small western gate. It was discovered by Peter de Roches, Bishop of Winchester, who rode with William Marshal. Marshal took the opportunity of a circuitous approach to Lincoln to bring news to the royalists that help was on its way.

The royalist army was accompanied by the legate Guala, who was prepared to excommunicate the French troops and absolve the English. Marshal addressed his troops, promising them honor and lifting their spirits. He was so eager to head to battle, his biographer notes, that he rode without his helmet and was called back to be properly armed. Marshal's bravery was also noted, as he was now over seventy years old. He used his massive size and his riding skills to thrust himself into combat.

The French and the barons had the advantage in numbers as they had twice as many knights. However, they were surprised by the determination of the loyalists as well as the presence of William Marshal. They were also pressed in between the castle walls they besieged and the cathedral that was behind them. General confusion and panic took over the rebel forces. Part of Louis' forces accompanied the barons with Count Perche as their commander. The count was killed by William Marshal, and the French troops decided to fall back after the loss of their commander. They eventually rallied and tried to rejoin the rebel forces, but they were now caught between Marshal and the main body of the royalist army. Over four hundred knights were taken as prisoners that day. Among them were the barons Fitzwalter and de Quincy.

Louis was now forced to negotiate with the royalists, as he alone stayed behind in London and was spared from the agony of the battle at Lincoln. Guala wished to severely punish Louis' ecclesiastical supporter Simon Langton, while Louis tried to protect him. The negotiations failed, and the French summoned reinforcements. It was Blanche of Castile, the granddaughter of Henry II and Louis' wife, who took it upon herself to gather the fleet and send it over the English Channel to help her husband. However, William Marshal sent Hubert de Burgh, Henry's justiciar, who intercepted the fleet off the coast of Sandwich and executed its captain as a common pirate. He then took the French reinforcements as prisoners. Louis was now forced to accept the terms offered to him during the negotiations. He renounced the throne and made an oath never to help the English rebels again. He did not leave England empty-handed, however. He was given an indemnity of 10,000 marks (almost £7,000 sterling) which was paid over a year. Louis also had to promise he would convince his father Philip, King of France, to return Henry's lands in France. Upon his arrival in France, Louis joined the Albigensian Crusade in the south of France. The barons were not severely punished either, and it was William Marshal who made sure the punishment was not too onerous. They were given amnesty, as well as freedom from all possible ransoms, and their lands were restored. Only the clergy who supported the rebellion didn't get back their lands, and that was considered punishment enough.

Later, reflecting on the events of First Barons' War, Henry III accused Marshal of betraying him by not punishing the barons and by not finishing off Louis. But Marshal stuck to his principles. He fought the war as a perfectly chivalrous knight, not as a bearer of royalist ideology. The rebelling barons were already excommunicated, and Marshal saw no reason to proclaim them traitors. Some historians see Marshal's decision not to punish the barons as a wise move. It helped heal the wounds England was left with due to the civil war. The power of the twenty-five was destroyed, as Fitzwalter and Quincy were beaten by the best knight in England, William Marshal. Even though the barons lost their power, the central ideas of the Magna Carta continued to live on through the reissued Great Charter of 1216.

# Chapter 7 – Henry III and the Magna Carta

Despite winning the First Barons' War, William Marshal faced great trouble while trying to restore royal authority throughout the country. Part of his inability lay in the fact that the barons who remained loyal to the Crown now asked for a reward after the civil war. William was unable to give them lands, as was the custom, because he had given them back to rebelling barons. Consequently, the Loyalists started showing less interest in the politics of the Crown, if not openly abandoning them. Furthermore, William tried to restore the Crown's right to approve marriages and wardships, but he failed. Where he was successful was in restoring the royal bench of judges and reopening the royal exchequer.

Henry's government issued the Charter of the Forest in 1217, which played a role in giving back the governance of the forests to the Crown. To the Normans who had ruled England since William the Conqueror, the forest was an enclosed area in which the king (and sometimes other aristocrats) had the exclusive right to hunt, cut wood, or use the grasslands, heathland or wetlands that were included in the common term "forest." Kings Richard and John started including more and more areas of England in the royal forest, expelling people who inhabited the areas or simply forbidding them to live off the land. At its widest, one-third of the land of southern England was assumed to be the royal forest.

Common people were forced to leave or die of starvation as they had no right to cultivate the lands or use it in any other way to sustain themselves.

The Charter of the Forest was issued together with the reissued Magna Carta as its complementary charter. Later it would be joined to the Magna Carta, but for now, it was a separate document that provided a certain degree of freedom and protection for the people who used the forest areas, mainly for their animals to graze or to grow their food. The first clause of the Forest Charter offered protection for all those who used the forest land as pastures for their animals and were already the inhabitants of the land. The ninth clause allowed all those who did not live in the areas of the forest to bring their livestock to graze in exchange for money. The Forest Charter also allowed people who lived in the forest area to build mills, fish preservation facilities, marl-pits, ditches, or gardens. The only condition was not to injure any neighboring lands. Clause ten banned the death penalty and mutilation as punishments for those who hunted in the forest. However, they still had to pay fines or face imprisonment.

By the times of the Tudors, the Forest Charter was mainly used to protect the timber industry and keep it in royal hands. Some clauses of this charter were enforced until 1970 through special courts that dealt with those who broke the law. The Forest Charter is the longest remaining medieval statute, as it was valid from 1217 until 1971. Finally, it was replaced with the still-active Wild Creatures and Forest Laws Act of 1971, which abolished the royal right to wild animals.

William Marshal fell ill in 1219 and believed he was dying. To prepare the new regency, he summoned the barons, Henry III, the papal legate Pandulf Verraccio, the royal justiciar Hubert de Burgh, and Peter des Roches, Bishop of Winchester. It was the Bishop who claimed the right of regency, but William refused him by appointing the papal legate, Verraccio. He had no trust in any of the aristocracy or clergy he summoned. William was invested into the order of the Knights Templar while on his deathbed due to his service in the crusade. He died on May 14, 1219, and was buried in the Temple Church in the London headquarters of the Templar Knights. His tomb can still be seen there and is open to visitors.

Pandulf Veraccio organized a new government around three ministers: himself, Peter de Roches, and Hubert de Burgh. They were appointed at Oxford by a great council of nobles. The new government had little success, as their authority was mainly dependent on this council of nobility. The bad luck of Henry III's government ended in 1220 when Pope Honorius III allowed Henry to be crowned for the second time. This act of renewed coronation had the purpose of strengthening the authority of the king. Barons, under the threat of excommunication, swore a new oath to Henry, promising they would repay their debts and give back the royal castles.

Meanwhile, Stephen Langton received the approval to return to England in 1219. However, it was not until 1221 that he regained the title of Archbishop of Canterbury. Langton returned to the political scene of England and took his seat at the triumvirate of councilors who guarded an under-aged king. It was two years later, in 1223 when King Henry III was finally proclaimed to be of the age to rule on his own. In January 1224, at Westminster Abbey, a council was held with Langton acting as spokesman for the barons. They called for the confirmation of the reissued Magna Carta, as it had already been sealed by the papal legate and the late regent, William Marshal. They were uncertain whether the king would ever acknowledge the Great Charter with his seals, and they insisted on reminding him.

Royal councilor William Brewer fought vigorously against the Magna Carta, claiming the liberties the barons demanded were extorted by force and therefore not valid. It was king Henry III who intervened to calm the situation that yet again threatened to divide his kingdom. He swore he would abide by the Great Charter, but he failed to give it a formal confirmation with royal seals.

In France, Louis VIII was now king, and he took advantage of Henry's weak government while he was still considered a minor by forcefully taking the remaining English lands on the continent, namely the provinces of Poitou and Gascony. To regain his territories, Henry needed money, and the royal council at Westminster approved a tax of £40,000 for the army. The barons issued a condition for Henry. They demanded he reissue the Magna Carta and the Charter of the Forest in exchange for their help. The king declared that the charters were given to the people with his free will and finally confirmed them with his royal seal on February 11th, 1225. The content of the reissued Great Charter was similar to that of the 1216 version, with some crucial differences.

In new words, the Magna Carta now gave the impression that it was solely the king's idea to reissue the Great Charter. This was a huge difference from the Charters of 1215 and 1216, which state the king approved of them by the advice of his councilors. In the 1225 version, there is no list of advisors or councilors that helped with the Magna Carta. There is only the king's name and those of the witnesses to the Charter. Among the mentioned witnesses are three loyalists who advised King John at Runnymede: the Earl of Salisbury, the Earl of Warenne, and Hubert de Burgh. Also, six of the barons who opposed John in the civil war were listed on the reissued Charter: Robert Fitzwalter, Gilbert de Clare, Hugh Bigod, Robert de Ros, Richard de Montfichet, and William d'Aubigny. William Brewer, a councilor who had opposed the Charter back in 1223, was now listed as a witness who endorsed the reissued version.

A new, final clause was added to the Magna Carta to explain the reason behind the reissuing.

"And for this our grant and gift of these liberties ... the archbishops, bishops, abbots, priors, earls, barons, knights, freeholders, and all of our realm have given us a fifteenth part of all their movables."[15]

After the Magna Carta was reissued, Stephen Langton threatened excommunication for anyone who violated it. Two years later, Langton managed to gain permission for his exiled brother Simon to come back to England. Having Simon—a very passionate supporter of the baronial movement back in 1215—to fight by his side, Stephen gained formal confirmation of the Great Charter by Pope Gregory IX in January 1228. The pope's admission of the Charter was very important for its sustainability, as he was still supreme pontiff and feudal overlord of England.

Langton died in July 1228. He was eighty years old but still had a very clear mind before his death. A man without whom the Magna Carta would never have existed, Langton was a great scholar and a reformer of the English church. History knows him for many deeds, such as opening the council at Osney, whose decrees from 1222 are known as the earliest provincial canons. But it was his achievement to bind the Magna Carta and the church together that is still regarded as his greatest feat.

When Henry III took the rule of his kingdom in his own hands, he realized the relationship of the Crown with the barons was not being repaired. He and the barons quarreled over the same issues they had during his father's reign. Henry showed the same unrealistic desire to regain his dynastic lands in France as his father had. He favored foreigners who inhabited his court, and many native nobles felt undesired and believed they did not have the protection of the law. The barons' role in the government started decreasing compared to their role during Henry's minority. Furthermore, Henry had the habit of bypassing the offices of the state that were run by domestic nobles, whose role was to limit the

---

[15] Magna Carta Translation, Final Clause. (n.d.). Retrieved from https://www.archives.gov/exhibits/featured-documents/magna-carta/translation.html

king's control over the kingdom. He relied on a home office, an administration that ran his household. While he continued to summon the royal council and Parliament during the 1230s, he preferred the advice of intimate friends from the court.

During the middle years of his reign, Henry III faced yet another barons' rebellion, which seemed to be a continuation of the civil war his father fought against. The barons wanted to revive the panel of twenty-five or organize a similar committee that would have a direct check on the king. They drew inspiration from the Magna Carta itself, and even though they failed at defending the liberties the Great Charter gave them, they managed to draw the public eye to it.

Once Henry III came of age and started ruling England on his own, his personality changed. He was often described as too pious, lazy, and overly trusting of his household. His views were often shaped by his advisors, and he was generally regarded as a naïve ruler. He was not able to exercise his own judgment on the propositions he was offered by his closest friends. He modeled his rule after King Edward the Confessor, who was proclaimed a saint but was hardly engaged in the rule of his own country. Henry compared his authority over England to the pope's authority over the church, relying too much on religious views and the sacramental characteristics of kings.

Because of this regard of kingship, Henry tried to evade the restrictions the Magna Carta imposed on him. He could not annul it, as it was the document that kept the barons satisfied, at least to some extent. Instead, he took it upon himself to appoint officials and patronage and make political decisions, as the Magna Carta did not give specific details on how the barons should be involved in such things. The barons felt excluded from the political world of their very own country, and they believed that Henry was acting against the Magna Carta. The reissued Magna Carta of 1225 was stripped of the security clause of John's Charter, and the barons and bishops were forced to search for other ways to enforce the Magna

Carta on the king. Henry wasn't concerned about the threats of excommunication that followed breaking the promises of the Magna Carta. He had the protection of the pope in Rome.

Henry III came into conflict with his justiciar, Hubert de Burgh, whose office in Westminster fought for the control of the government. In 1232, Henry removed Hubert from the office and had him arrested and his lands confiscated. Peter des Roches, the bishop of Winchester who was a passionate advocate for the authoritarian administration of John's rule, became the king's favorite advisor. It was des Roches who urged Henry to recover the lost French lands of his dynasty, but the endeavors in Poitou failed (1230-1242). Although he did regain Gascony, Henry lost other oversea territories that had been under English rule until then.

Henry III brought the foreign mercenaries he'd hired back to England and would not send them home. He continued to pay them, and he gave lands and castles to foreign nobles who enjoyed privileges in his court. To grant the lands to foreign magnates, Henry first had to take them away from domestic nobles, who were also des Roches' political opponents, and by doing so, he undermined the basis of landholding laws. It was this behavior that started a great crisis in 1232. Eventually, this crisis would result in another reaffirmation of the Magna Carta.

The first to complain about the king's new policies was Richard Marshal, son of William Marshal and the 3rd Earl of Pembroke. A new civil war broke out with Peter des Roches on one side and Richard Marshal and his followers on the other. During this revolt, Henry III was unable to gain military advantage over the united rebels, and he started to fear that Louis of France would come back to England and take advantage of the unrest in England to seize even more territories for France. The Archbishop of Canterbury summoned several great councils during 1234, in which he tried to persuade Henry to dismiss des Roches. Finally, des Roches was disgraced, and Henry agreed to peace.

Henry III did learn a lesson or two from the crisis that shook England from 1232 to 1234. He was reminded that the Magna Carta had the power to place him under the law and that earls, barons, and bishops were willing to judge him. Hubert de Burgh was restored as justiciar, and the king had to return the lands to the nobles who were injured during de Roches' service as the king's advisor.

It seems that King Henry III did not learn his lessons from this crisis until the end. The barons were right to be afraid of the king's subsequent behavior. Henry continued to interfere in lawsuits against tenants, even though the Magna Carta guaranteed them the liberties of their courts. After 1234, there was a lack of general justice in the kingdom, as Henry denied or delayed the prosecution of his close royal officials. Again, among those who enjoyed the king's protection were his foreign friends of the court–for example, the uncles to his wife, Eleanor of Provence, or his Lusignan half-brothers who were seeking their fortune in England. Once more, the native barons were left aside, feeling unwelcome at the royal court and outside of the law. Henry also allowed corruption to grow among the judges of his court, as he would often turn a blind eye toward the crimes his family and friends committed.

In the countryside, however, Henry III could not impose order, and local leaders rose to power. The barons were left to deal with the peacekeeping of their counties as the royal sheriff network collapsed. Domestic nobles lost all respect they had for their king, especially after he proved to be an incompetent military commander by losing all French territories by 1253. Throughout his military campaigns, Henry was always in need of money but was unable to persuade the barons to consent to money-grants due to a lack of capable advisors. The only thing he was capable of doing was raising taxes, as advised by his foreign friends. He exploited the Jews with heavy tallages, or land taxes, which resulted in the destruction of the Jewish community in medieval England. He also indulged in repossessing alienated royal lands to finance his war. He exploited the royal forest, which was protected by the Forest Charter. Instead of gathering enough money to finance his army in France, Henry III only managed to agitate his subjects, who saw his behavior as yet another violation of the Magna Carta. The barons insisted that Henry should reaffirm the Magna Carta in 1253, and in return, they promised financial aid for his campaign in Gascony. But it proved that this time, reaffirmation wasn't enough, as Henry continued abusing his rule.

Due to Henry's inept rule, a new crisis arose in the 1250s that inspired a new major reform movement among the nobles and clergy. The two groups were pulled together, as piety penetrated noble society. The clergy had a huge role in focusing the attention of the new rebellion to the Magna Carta. In 1258, the Archbishop of Canterbury openly accused Henry of violation of the churches' liberties, and those granted by the Magna Carta. Specifically, they claimed Henry kept ecclesiastical positions open so that he could enjoy the income they were bringing, as the king took it upon himself to appoint church officials. They continued pointing out how this behavior violated the Magna Carta on three occasions. The church also wanted to be involved in episcopal elections, as they saw elections as their domain. The Great Charter of King John granted the freedom of election to the church, a point which even Pope Innocent III embraced.

On the other hand, the barons were offended by how Henry III dealt with the distribution of patronage. They saw the king granting lands and castles to foreigners instead of domestic nobles. Even royal officials were alarmed when the king started granting large portions of land that were bringing income to the Crown to his half-brothers and his wife's uncles, the foreigners. This resulted in the dissipation of the Crown's resources, and the royal administrators could not ignore it. There were even suspicions of a secret government that ruled from within the royal household since the justiciar position had remained vacant since 1232. Also, the royal chancellor was no longer in charge of the royal seal since, in 1238, Henry took the responsibility on himself. Once more, the failings of the king cried for the reaffirmation of the Magna Carta, but it wouldn't be enough. The barons were left powerless, and they did not influence the king's choice to appoint royal officials.

It was the "Sicilian Business" that proved Henry III had a bad habit of listening to the flawed council of his foreign relatives and friends. In 1254, Henry accepted the offer from the pope to take over Sicily and gift its throne to his second son, Edward. Pope Innocent IV was in a personal vendetta war with the Hohenstaufen family, which had imperial authority over Italy. To speed up the arrival of Henry's army in Sicily, the Pope offered Henry a large sum of money, which he invested in the campaign. But soon after, Innocent was succeeded with Alexander IV, who refused to pay for Henry's campaign. Instead, he demanded Henry return the money he was given by Innocent. The sum was enormous, totaling £90,000, and Henry was unable to pay it. He turned to Parliament, asking for the barons' help, but they refused him. He attempted to gain Parliament's assistance for three more years, but Alexander was unhappy with the delay, so he sent an envoy to England threatening to excommunicate the king if he couldn't pay his debts to Rome. Parliament yet again refused to help Henry, who started extorting the money out of the senior clergy. He made them sign blank charters, which he then used as a promise that they would assist the king in raising the money for the efforts in Italy. In this way, he gathered around £40,000. The war in Italy had no support from his nobles and thus culminated in open revolt in 1258.

# Chapter 8 –Second Barons' War and Edward I

The revolt started when seven barons formed an alliance with the goal of expelling King Henry III's half-brothers, the Lusignans, out of England. Among them was even a foreigner, Simon de Montfort, Earl of Leicester, who was French by origin. He married the king's sister and gained titles, but soon after, he fell out of the king's grace. His motivation for joining the revolt might have been personal, but he became the loudest advocate of reforms that would be beneficial not only to the barons but also to the knight class. Knights were also suffering as the government isolated the king, who allowed profit and financial advantages only to the people closest to him. Other barons who forged the alliance with them were Roger and Hugh Bigod, John Fitzgeoffrey, Peter de Montfort, Peter de Savoy, and Richard de Clare. These seven barons also gained the support of Queen Eleanor, who saw benefits in expelling the Lusignans out of the kingdom.

The baron's revolt of 1258 is considered the second great crisis in the rule of Henry III. They sought, once more, to restrain the king's authority, and they wished to move beyond the Magna Carta and secure permanent baronial involvement in the government, to control the king and put him under the rule of law. They also wished to reform the state offices so that they would start serving the kingdom, not just the king. The barons started the revolt slowly by showing up at Parliament sessions often to voice their demands and express their views of the kingship. After a relatively short time, the seven barons started demanding the changes with aggression, and Henry could no longer deny the danger of a new civil war. However, the barons faced a dilemma. There was nothing in their power to make the king accept the reforms if they wished to avoid violence, which could mark them as oath breakers and have them arrested for treason. They decided to treat the king as a mentally ill, incompetent ruler whose advisors needed to be changed. They sought to return the body of the councilors as the king's guardians, just as in the years of his minority. The barons formed "*le commun de Engleterre,*" or, as translated in modern English, "the community of the realm," a society that had the power to speak for the whole kingdom.

In June 1258, during the parliament session in Oxford, a demand was presented that the king should be faithful to the oath he made while reissuing the Magna Carta in 1225. Parliament proceeded with the insistence that both the king and the "community of the realm" should form a committee that would reform the government. Each party had to nominate twelve representatives, who would become the members of the committee and would work together to construct the acceptable reforms. This committee started their work and issued a series of governmental experiments that would last until 1265. They concentrated on searching for a way to limit the king's power and broadened the responsibilities of the English government. The measures passed by this parliament meeting are known as the Provisions of Oxford.

The committee came up with the idea of two councils that would share the power with the king. One would consist of fifteen officials chosen in equal numbers by the king and by the barons. The other council would be made of twelve who would be appointed by the barons alone. Their role would be to deal with the common laws and the business of the kingdom and the king. The barons wanted the full restoration of the justiciary and chancellor's offices, but they also demanded that these offices be separated from the king's household. The next to undergo reform would have been the office of the exchequer, which would prevent the king from shifting the financial flow toward his household. However, the implementation of such a reform would take away the king's executive power and reduce him to a puppet monarch.

In the protests of Henry's rule, the Magna Carta was often cited, mostly by the clergy, who shaped the revolt into a moral crusade. They also shamed the nobles into joining them by calling them "modern princes who oppress poor folk."[16]. Minor nobles, knights, and freeholders joined the barons and urged for reforms in local governments. The desire for change spread throughout the whole kingdom, including the countryside. In October 1259, the knights were granted the Provisions of Westminster, which reaffirmed the Magna Carta and the Forest Charter. It limited the office of the sheriff to native knights who were to be elected annually and who would receive a salary for the job. The Provisions also restricted the authority of magnates in their courts, granting liberties to all free men who were the subjects of their jurisdictions. This clause always existed in the Magna Carta, but it was never implemented until 1259 when the council of twelve heard the complaints of the common people.

Cooperation between the king and the council was impossible, and the new constitution lasted for only two years. It collapsed in April 1261, when Henry III wrote to the pope asking for absolution from the oaths with which he supported the decisions of Parliament. To appease the people, the king tried to reassure them that he would still respect the charters, both the Magna Carta and the Charter of the Forest. However, Henry started replacing sheriffs who were elected by the barons, and he took control over some of

[16] Carpenter (1999), 339; Maddicot (1994), 353-5.

the royal castles. The barons, with Simon de Montfort as their leader, once more united and started a government that would operate independently of the king. This time, they did not have the support of the queen, who helped her husband raise a mercenary army. Threatened by civil war, the barons were forced to back down. Simon was exiled to France, and the resistance of the barons was over, for the moment. Henry continued abusing his power by bullying his political opposition and extorting money from the Jews with high taxes. He continued to enjoy his authority over the kingdom until 1263, when the pope decided to reverse his judgment of the Oxford and Westminster Provisions, confirming their legitimacy. The country easily slipped back into civil war, as the barons believed they had the support of Rome.

Simon de Montfort was now able to return to England and gather the rebelling barons around him. The civil war broke out in October of 1263 between King Henry III, who had the support of his son Edward, and the loyalist barons and de Montfort, backed by the radically-oriented nobility. The rebels persuaded knights to join their cause, and together they started disposing of the evidence of their debts to the Jews to avoid paying them. As the Jews were considered the property of the Crown, the returned loans would end up in the king's hands. Five hundred Jews died when London rose in revolt. The rebels managed to completely replace the royal household of intimate friends of the king who acted as his councilors.

The war dragged on, and Montfort's victory at the Battle of Lewes in 1264 seemed to be the decisive battle. Montfort took complete control over the government, but he could not get rid of the king, as he was an anointed monarch. His authority had no legitimacy. The only path Simon de Montfort could take was to rule in the name of King Henry III, whom he held captive. To broaden his support, he ordered four knights from each county to come to the parliament sessions. He did not include only the knights in

Parliament; he also invited merchants, thus widening the definition of the community in the kingdom.

Simon did not rule for long since some barons saw him as an obstacle to making peace with the king. He could not keep his followers united, and soon, some defected. Only a year after the Battle of Lewes, the royalist army defeated the reformist barons at Evesham, and it took only a few days for Henry III to nullify all the reforms implemented by Montfort. Simon Montfort was killed during the battle, and the barons no longer had anyone to unify them behind their cause.

The Second Barons' War failed to restrict the king's power. However, the Magna Carta was still at the very center of English law and politics. The king issued the Dictum of Kenilworth in 1266, with which he pronounced the reconciliation of the rebels. Once again, Henry III made a promise that he would abide by the Magna Carta and the Forest Charter. The king's heir, Lord Edward, became the de facto ruler alongside his father. He had sympathy for some of the reforms executed in 1259, and he secured the enactment of these reforms with the Statute of Marlborough. The Magna Carta was included in this statute, as Edward confirmed that all articles of the Great Charter would be respected equally, whether they concerned the king or the people.

However, once he became the sole king of the realm, Edward I governed England in the same manner as his father and grandfather. He strictly followed the Angevin tradition of preserving and expanding royal power. However, unlike his predecessors, Edward succeeded in bolstering the Crown's position as he enjoyed his rights to the fullest extent. One major difference between Henry III and Edward was that the later came to the throne as an adult, already having vast experience in how to govern. He was more capable of maintaining an efficient administration even through warfare, which was characteristic of his rule. He was determined to defend Gascony, the last English possession in France. He also tried to extend the English kingdom by taking over the whole British island. Of course, all this warfare demanded revenue-raising measures, which again oppressed and angered his subjects. In the last decade of his rule, a resistance formed once again and asked for the confirmation of the charters.

Edward I was, for a long time, considered an image of a strong and righteous monarch and the ideal image of a ruler, as he was a warrior-king who transformed the English administration and common law and was also known for his Christian piety and chivalry. However, modern historians believe that if he had ruled for just a bit longer, Edward would've turned England into an absolute monarchy, such as France was. As it stands, Edward is considered one of the fathers of the English Parliament, which finally settled on having regular sessions. Edward's parliament saw fit to replace the baronial committees with knights and townspeople who acted as spokesmen of their social classes. But this parliament also served as a body that allowed the king to legally raise taxes whenever he wished. The wars Edward was so eager to fight cost a lot more than a 13th-century king could afford.

The first time Edward confirmed the Magna Carta and the Forest Charter was in 1276, which resulted in a lack of any kind of political crisis that would disturb the early years of his reign. This period is often highlighted by historians as the high point of Medieval England.

In the second part of his rule, in his mature years, Edward's government violated the spirit of the Magna Carta. His problems were always financial, as he often fought wars on multiple fronts, engaging himself against France, the Scots, and the Welsh. During the 1290s, it seemed as if there were no end to Edward's military campaigns, and he imposed heavy taxation on the kingdom to keep financing his armies. A once-popular king was now resented by his own people. A political crisis erupted in 1297 when the barons, clergy, bishops, and merchants formed an opposition. Once again, the Magna Carta had the spotlight in the political turmoil of England. Parliament used the Magna Carta as a weapon, demanding that it be confirmed and reworked, as some of the clauses required clarification. They asked for supplementary clauses which would impose the rule of law on the king in hopes it would end his constant demand for higher taxes.

During the 13th century, the Great Charter—the Magna Carta—was a widely known document, as every lawyer or landholder had a copy of it and used it as a legal handbook. All the classes who owned some property were especially attracted to the Magna Carta. They could grasp its significance, as it had clauses that defended their rights and liberties. The ecclesiastic order valued the Great Charter because it guaranteed the church's freedom, and it is no wonder that the clergy were the first to oppose Edward's abuse of power.

Edward I used church funds (around half of its income) to reward his royal clerks, and this was the reason for the quarrel between the king and the Archbishop of Canterbury, who wanted to reform the church. The Archbishop organized the reading of the Magna Carta during the ecclesiastic council, after which he threatened excommunication for anyone who violated the freedom of the English church. He also ensured that all people could have access to the Great Charter and ordered its display in all cathedrals and churches. On Edward's orders, these copies of the Magna Carta were taken down as a clear sign of his resentment toward the Archbishop's decisions. The English clergy appealed to Pope Boniface VIII, who was eager to show his dominance over Edward, who ruled as a secular monarch. In 1296, the pope issued a bull that forbade the king from taxing the church and the clergy without the permission of the pontiff. The English clergy hoped for a different outcome, as this papal bull threw them into a dilemma. They were now either to disobey their secular ruler—the king—or the pope himself. They chose to disobey Edward, who used the opportunity to place them outside of royal protection. This meant they were now outlaws. In the end, the pope agreed to a compromise in 1297 that allowed rulers to tax the clergy without papal permission but only in times of emergency. However, the pop never defined what would be considered an emergency, so the monarchs were free to come to their own conclusions.

Edward I did not fail to anger the merchants either. He raised the customs taxes, which remained known as *maltote*, or evil toll, as named by the people of that time. In July of 1294, the king ordered an increase of the tax on all moveable wealth. He also made merchants sell wool to him, and then the Crown would resell it for a much higher profit used to fund the war. He also angered the barons by ordering them to fight in Flanders, where the barons had no interests of their own and their ancestors had never set foot before, a land to which they had no ties or any reason to fight for.

The resentment of the opposition was so great that Edward took care to reinforce the royal castles in case the civil war broke out while he was on his campaign in Flanders. Dissatisfaction with how high the tolls were resulted in two earls bringing their armies to the exchequer, forbidding the office to collect taxes. Edward I left his son and heir, Edward Caernarvon, to deal with the crisis that rose in England. In October 1297, he summoned Parliament, promising the confirmation of the Magna Carta and the Forest Charter. However, the barons insisted on adding new clauses to the Magna Carta that would limit the king's power, and Edward had to refuse them. Instead, the clauses were published in a separate document that contained six promises known as the Confirmation of the Charters. The first clause made Edward promise to keep the Magna Carta and the Forest Charter, as confirmed by his father, Henry III. Another clause said that the charters needed to be sent to all cathedrals, where they would be read to the people twice a year. Three years later, in 1300, as the war with the Scots raged on and Edward tried to raise taxes once more, the bishops had the Magna

Carta confirmed once again. This confirmation of the Charter is important in history because it was the first time it was read to people in the English language.

Edward I did manage to free himself of the confirmation of the Magna Carta of 1300 by making a deal with the merchants, who agreed on increased customs in 1303. An agreement made with only one group instead of the whole community during a parliament session violated the spirit of the Magna Carta. However, the king went even further and made a deal with the pope. He was granted absolution from the promises presented in the Confirmation of the Charters in exchange for consent to the pope's levy of a tax on the English church. Even though the king disavowed the Confirmation of the Magna Carta, it remained in the memory of his subjects, and they pressed hard on their monarch for new confirmations.

The legal profession started emerging in the $14^{th}$ century, and it gave the Magna Carta a pivotal place in English law. Lawyers of the late medieval age, who practiced outside of universities, resented canon and Roman law and instead glorified the Magna Carta since it was the native English law.

# Chapter 9 – The Late Medieval Period and the Tudors

Henry VII, Founder of the Tudor Dynasty

(Source:https://en.wikipedia.org/wiki/House_of_Tudor#/media/File:Enrique_VII_de_Inglaterra,_por_un_artista_an%C3%B3nimo.jpg)

The Magna Carta continued to be confirmed throughout the 13th and 14th centuries, but later it was shadowed by high politics and remained in the background until the 17th century. The rapid economic changes and endemic lawlessness that marked the period had a higher priority for the barons than the Magna Carta. However, the Magna Carta wasn't entirely forgotten. It was confirmed eight times during the 15th century, which is, nevertheless, significantly lower than the thirty confirmations it had received in the previous century. The Great Charter continued to be observed in parliamentary and judicial proceedings during the late Middle Ages. During the reign of Edward III (1327-77), six statutes were enacted, and they defined the Charter's promise of what was to become the "due process of law." The Magna Carta was used to teach the common law tradition of due process, not only to lawyers but also to the country's gentry. Legal expertise was essential for the landholding class, and it started to realize this. Landholders considered the Magna Carta and the common law to be the best protectors of property rights.

The English Parliament had taken shape during the reign of Edward I, but it was in the times of Edward III that it went through key stages of development. When Parliament allowed spokesmen for the ranks bellow the barons and nobles, it became the protector of the liberties promised to the people by the Magna Carta. During the 14th century, each first petition of the parliament session was made by the House of Commons, which requested that the Great Charter and the Charter of the Forest be firmly followed.

The Magna Carta, the Forest Charter, and the Confirmation of the Charters of Edward I were considered sacred during the 14th century. Statutes that opposed this document were regarded as invalid. The practice continued during the reign of Edward III, who even called for the examination of the statutes to confirm they did not oppose the Magna Carta.

The reign of Edward II reversed the kingdom to the times of Henry III with the practice of a household government. Edward II was known for lavishing his friends with gifts in the form of money and lands with no regard for how useful these people were to the politics of the kingdom. Once more, the barons gathered to devise a plan on how to supervise the government. Personal rivalries obscured the importance of the Magna Carta and constitutional principles. Both factions, royalists and reformists, were prepared to take up arms and fight for control over the king and the government. Armed conflict erupted when the king refused to exile his closest friend Piers Gaveston, the first Earl of Cornwall, who had an enormous influence on the politics of England. In fact, contemporary chroniclers have said that, at the time, England was ruled by two kings, Edward II and Gaveston—one by name and the other by actions. It is said that Edward II preferred the company of his friend Gaveston to the company of his wife, Queen Isabella. It is no wonder she gave her support to the reformist barons. The king had to send his friend into exile in 1308, appointing him Lieutenant of Ireland. At the same time, he wrote to Pope Clement V, requesting that Gaveston be allowed to return to England. The Earl of Cornwall was permitted to return to England, but his relationship with the barons proved to be very difficult. Soon, his political enemies refused to be present in parliament meetings just because he was there. The barons petitioned King Edward to abandon Gaveston as his councilor and to instead admit the advisory body of twenty-one elected barons known as the Lords Ordainers, or simply Ordainers. Their goal was to carry out reform of both the government and the royal household. Edward accepted, and the Ordainers were elected from both the reformist faction and the royalists. They came up with a series of ordinances in 1311 for reordering the government. The Magna Carta had an important role in the construction of these ordinances. Articles 6 and 38 acknowledged that the monarch was bound by the Great Charter and that he would keep all points of the Magna Carta. The Charter was made as a standard for legislation in Article 31, which points out that if any statute conflicts with the Magna Carta or the Charter of the Forest, it is to be annulled.

Under the Ordinances of 1311, Edward was still the head of the government and chief of state, and he considered the Ordinances to be crippling to his royal executive power. When Gaveston was captured and killed by the barons, Edward was determined to gain release from the Ordinances. However, to secure a campaign in Scotland, he agreed to forgive the barons involved in Gaveston's death and to uphold the Ordinances. The king was quick to find a new favorite, Hugh Despenser the Younger, whose influence and acquisition of lands in Wales angered the barons once more. Edward II granted his army to Despenser in his land grab on the Welsh borders. The barons considered this move a direct violation of Clauses 29 and 39 of the Magna Carta, as the king was sending the army against his subjects. In 1321, Despenser's enemies occupied most of the parliament seats, and a vote to exile him and his father from England passed. The king tried to defend his favorite, calling on the Magna Carta because banishing Despenser "would be contrary to the common law of our realm."[17] At the Battle of Boroughbridge in 1322, the king's army defeated the baronial party, and the travesties of the trials similar to the one that exiled Despenser repeated. Twenty-five barons were executed, while others were either imprisoned or fined for the roles they took against the king. The Magna Carta's guarantee that punishment must be a result of judgment was ignored, as trials by peers were not conducted. After these events, the Magna Carta grew in its importance once more.

The Parliament in York cited the Magna Carta's law of the land, and Despenser's exile was revoked. The Statute of York refused to acknowledge the Ordinances of 1311 and concluded that it was not the barons who knew what was best for the king and the kingdom. This revocation of the Ordinances did not influence the validity of the Great Charter, which continued to be reaffirmed when the

---

[17] Thompson, Faith (1948), *Magna Carta: its role in the making of the English constitution, 1300-1629*, Minneapolis: University of Minnesota Press.,78.

occasion demanded it. Eventually, Edward II was forced to abdicate due to the political schemes of his own wife, Queen Isabelle of France, and her lover Roger Mortimer. The pair placed the king's underage son, Edward III, on the throne while they ruled as regents.

Once eighteen, Edward III took the kingdom into his own hands and banished his mother while executing Mortimer. His rule was one of warfare: he started the Hundred Years War (1338-1453) as he tried to recover the Plantagenet lands in France. The barons shared his enthusiasm for war, and as long as the king was giving royal privileges to the Parliament, the barons were happy to finance the war. They were also eager to recover the lands in France, which would bring them more prospects.

Edward III was succeeded by his grandson Richard II, whose rule was often described as weak, much like the rules of Henry III and Edward II, since they all held a household parliament filled with bad advisors. Like his two predecessors, Richard was forced to share executive power with the barons. He accepted the reform commission of 1386, known as the Lords Appellant, which resembled the Lords Ordainers of Edward II. At the time, the Hundred Years War was raging, but Richard was a king who sought peace. His barons were unsatisfied with his decision to pursue peace because they profited greatly from the war with France. In Richard II's later rule, it seems that the Magna Carta was forgotten. It continued to exist–it was never annulled, and lawyers continued to use it as a handbook for common law. But the citizens had lost their trust in common law, and while petitioning the king or Parliament, they never cited the Magna Carta. Even during the Peasants' Revolt in 1381, when the people made demands for their personal freedoms, they did not once call on the Magna Carta.

Richard II devoted himself to getting rid of Parliament's decision to share power with the Lords Appellant, and by 1388, he succeeded. After gaining all the executive power for himself, the king started a despotic rule. His enemies were either exiled or executed, and none of them were inspired by persecution to appeal to the Magna Carta's protection. Richard enforced his military tribunals, and the Court of the Constable and traditional common law courts were forgotten. During the totalitarian phase of his regime, King Richard II disinherited his own cousin, Henry Bolingbroke, who was exiled and whose lands and estates were confiscated. This action directly threatened the property rights of the aristocracy and pushed the magnates into rebellion. Richard was forced to face the rebels alone since he had no one's support. In 1399, Parliament started the process of disposition, forcing Richard to abdicate. Still, it was done in such a manner as to leave the impression that the king had abdicated of his own free will. Since Richard had no son, his closest relative who succeeded him was the same Henry Bolingbroke whom he had exiled. Bolingbroke was crowned Henry IV, first of the Lancastrian kings.

Periodic confirmation of the Magna Carta, which grew into a custom, ended during the reign of Henry VI, the last Lancastrian king. Historians explain that the importance of the Great Charter waned as England became a country of disorder and political disasters. But the Magna Carta was not forgotten. There is plenty of evidence that the Charter was cited and that defendants were appealing to its technical provisions. Also, lawyers and judges cited it for their occasional petty purposes. Appeals to the Charter's guarantee of due process are nonexistent during the times of the Lancastrian and Yorkist kings. The political scene where lawlessness ruled and the constant danger of coups d'état were fertile grounds for the kings' constant violations of Clauses 29 and 39. Amidst the changes that the 15th century brought, the Magna Carta was not in the center of political life anymore. Edward IV and Richard III, together with their Tudor successors, were often accused by their contemporaries of leading England to modern absolutism.

The councilor or prerogative courts of the Tudor times threatened the common law courts' existence. They were more efficient in enforcing law and order than the traditional common law courts were ever able to. Another downside of the common law courts was the corruption of the judges and the easy intimidation of the juries. With authoritarian procedures derived from Roman law, the tribunals were designed to bring swift justice, punish offenses that the common law prohibited, and strike awe and fear into the magnates.

Under the rule of the Tudors, the Magna Carta continued to be in the back of the political scene of England. Starting in 1399, the kingdom had a series of weak rulers, and the need for a strong government rose. Many people thought that sacrificing a few of their liberties was a small price to pay for a stable and orderly kingdom. With Henry VII and his successors came the Tudor despotism, and these rulers represent early examples of absolute monarchy, which was customary for 16th and 17th century Europe. However, today's historians believe that the Tudors could never exercise a truly despotic rule for the simple fact that they lacked resources. Besides lacking money, the Tudors had no standing army or a force that could police the country. They, too, depended on the support of the barons and state magnates to raise taxes. The Tudors were aware that the Crown had to keep the appearance of acknowledging due process, and in return, the judges and lawyers protected the Crown's privilege in the court.

When Henry VIII made the Anglican church independent from Rome, he violated the rights of his subjects. This only serves to show how little the Magna Carta was respected during his rule. He often imprisoned his political opponents without pressing any charges just to show his power over them. Only occasionally someone would call on the Magna Carta, claiming his rights and liberties as an Englishman. Even though the first clause of the Great Charter guaranteed the freedom of the English church, most of the

Catholics who were persecuted by the king turned to the pope and his authority for arguments against royal supremacy. To understand why no aristocratic magnate rose in opposition to the rule of the Tudors, one must realize the atmosphere of their rule.

The English social and economic structure was no longer medieval, and the aristocracy lost their political influence. The rapid economic changes of the 16th century left the barons in confusion, and they were barely capable of adapting. Commerce replaced agriculture as a source of wealth, while inflation was rising and the expenses of a luxury life became unaffordable for many. The poverty the barons suddenly experienced drove them to flock around the king in hopes of earning his patronage. While the fortune of the aristocrats was falling, the gentry—the descendants of the medieval knights—were rising. Many of them won the election and became members of the House of Commons, and they finally started expressing their own political and religious concerns.

Another novelty of the 16th century was a cultural current from Italy known as humanism. The idea of a perfect gentleman who had the qualities of a medieval chivalric knight and knowledge of Greek and Roman philosophy occupied the minds of not only the aristocracy but also the gentry. Tudor subjects were living in a new age free from the chaos of civil war with a new, rejuvenated monarchy, enjoying the new teachings of humanism. Liberated from the papal grasp on their religion, the people of England saw no point in rebelling over the few liberties that were taken away from them.

With the invention of the printing press and the kingdom's thirst for knowledge, the Magna Carta returned to England's attention. Copies of it were printed as early as the 1480s, and together with other legal textbooks, the Great Charter was among the first books to be printed in the Kingdom of England. The first time the Magna Carta was published in full was in 1508 by an immigrant from Normandy, Richard Pynson, who became the "king's official printer." His prints of *Magna Carta, cum aliis antiquis statutis* became the most reprinted edition and the basis for the modern English translation.

Around the same time, due to humanism, an interest in England's history awoke. For the first time, people became aware of the controversy that followed King John and the signing of the Magna Carta. Until now, they had known the Great Charter only from the statute books and only its version from 1225. The 1215 version of the Charter became known through the work of Archbishop of Canterbury Matthew Parker, who gathered medieval manuscripts and held one of the most important collections, which he left to the University Library of Cambridge College. But the first printer to publish the translated version of the Magna Carta was George Ferrers, in 1579. Ferrers was a politician, poet, and a common lawyer who printed the full text of the Charter in English, not Latin. His translation is often clumsy, as he used more words than needed to describe certain terms. However, he did convey the general meaning of the document.

The recovery of the Magna Carta's version from 1215 shed new light on the dispute King John had with his barons, and the contemporary texts were often biased and openly supported the rebellion. However, the English public still avoided questions concerning the monarchy, English constitution, and English liberties. They were aware that the discussion of such issues was dangerous at a time when Tudors held England in their royal grip. There was no opposition strong enough to question the character of a Tudor's monarchy, no one brave enough to allow himself to be inspired by the Barons' Revolt and reclaim those liberties.

The meaning of the Magna Carta was, perhaps, most clearly grasped by the Puritans, who were under constant pressure for religious compliance under Elizabeth I. Some even argued that the first clause of the Magna Carta, which guaranteed the freedom of the "English Church," did not apply only to the Anglican church, but to all. The lawyers who took the cases of the Puritans resurrected the promises of the Great Charter, and pamphlets publicizing the liberties it guaranteed started circulating the country. Robert Beale and James Morice, both members of Parliament, composed treatises describing the Magna Carta as basic and unchangeable law–the law above all royal writs, the law of law. This upholding of the Magna Carta by the Puritans and their representatives prepared the way for the parliamentarians of the 17th century, who would use the Magna Carta against the Stuart monarchy that succeeded the Tudors.

# Chapter 10 – The Revival of the Magna Carta

During the 17th century, the Magna Carta once more took a central place in the political and royal life of the English kingdom. The parliamentarians and common lawyers used the Great Charter to fight the royal prerogative reasserted by James I. During the 17th century in Europe, the trend was to support the divine right of the monarch. Considering modern European values, the Magna Carta was an anomaly, with its tradition of subjecting royal power to the rule of law. Queen Elizabeth I, the last ruler of the House of Tudor, was succeeded by James VI of Scotland, who upon being crowned, ruled as James I of England. Accustomed to the notion of a divine-right monarchy, he had little trouble adapting to Tudor authoritarianism. However, the combination of totalitarian notions in one monarch threatened Parliament's role in governing the kingdom. By the 1640s, the monarch's opponents faced the same problems as the barons of King John. They needed a solution for a king who refused to respect the law. As the problem was the same as in 1215, so was the answer: civil war. This time, instead of the barons, the leaders were parliamentarians, and the result of the 1642-48 civil war was far more eccentric. The king was executed, and England fell into a decade of experimental republican government.

The rule of the Stuart kings that led to the civil war during the reign of Charles I is comparable to the rule of King John, Henry III, and Edward I. James I issued a patent for monopoly over the trade of certain goods. He privileged his favorites, and the competition was often imprisoned for infringement. The victims understood such actions violated Clauses 29/39 of the Magna Carta. James canceled some of the monopolies to appease his opponents, but that wasn't enough. In 1624, Parliament issued a statute that limited royal monopolies. To raise revenues without Parliament's consent, the Stuart kings often turned to purveyance (the right of sovereigns to buy provisions at a fixed price that was much lower than the market value). Protests followed such actions, and the members of the House of Commons of the English Parliament cited the Magna Carta in their fight against the royals. However, the protests achieved nothing, as the House of Lords did not want to provoke King James. Avoiding any conflict, Parliament decided to ignore the pleas of the Commons.

The Puritans continued their fight against the monarchs over the supervision of the church of England. Both Elizabeth I and her Stuart successors considered authority over the church to be their royal prerogative. However, Puritans, who were occupying more and more seats in the House of Commons, challenged this prerogative. They wanted total eradication of Papism and reconstruction of the Anglican church based on their own belief system. They named themselves Puritans as they sought to "purify" the church from the influence of Roman Catholic practices and finally turn it to clear Protestantism.

In the early 1620s, the members of the House of Commons demanded that their king, Charles I, reaffirm the Magna Carta. It was Sir Edward Coke—a lawyer, judge, and politician—who claimed that the Magna Carta was still valid when the king started to imprison those who refused to pay forced loans and taxes. Charles I was willing to confirm the Great Charter but refused to allow its reinterpretation. However, this did not please the Commons, who answered by issuing the Petition of Right, which asked for specific liberties for the English people, such as the restriction of taxation which did not gain Parliament's approval, forced billeting of soldiers, imprisonment without charge, and use of martial law. Clauses 29/39 of the Magna Carta took a central place in the Petition of Right. When it reached the House of Lords, some fully supported it, but others sought to change it and preserve some of the royal prerogatives. The Lords proposed a version of the petition that would be a compromise; however, the Commons, with Coke as their leader, strongly opposed it. When the petition reached Charles I, he had no choice but to accept it. Soon after, he broke his promises and started arresting members of the Commons without offering any reason. Many did not survive imprisonment and could not raise any objections. Charles I started his tyrannical rule, and Parliament did not assemble for the next eleven years, from 1629 until 1640.

Charles was convinced he could be a good ruler if he only wasn't constricted by Parliament, but he soon faced the problem of finding new revenue streams without Parliament's grants. To deal with this problem, Charles continued to break the promises of not only the Magna Carta but also the Forest Charter by trying to extend the royal forests. He also exploited payments for coastal defense by extending its parameters to the whole kingdom, exclaiming that the entirety of England benefited from the royal navy. All these sources of revenue allowed him to collect enough money to enjoy times of peace. However, the king provoked a conflict in Scotland, and it was soon clear that the income was not enough. The king tried to force Anglican teachings on the Scottish church, which resulted in war in 1639/40. War debts forced the king to summon Parliament once more.

The first parliament session in 1640, known as the Short Parliament since it lasted for only three weeks, did not want to solve the king's financial issues until he granted his subjects assured liberties. The Magna Carta was once more at the center of attention, and the king could not gain control over Parliament. It had to be disbanded. The second parliament session, known as the Long Parliament, followed soon after and would exist until 1653 when Oliver Cromwell dissolved it. However, this Parliament had no more interest in solving the king's problems than the previous did.

It was this Parliament that sought to restrain the king's absolute power by trying to take control of the military from the king's hands. In 1641, there was a massive uprising in Ireland against the Protestants, and the king needed an army to deal with it. However, Parliament was reluctant, as they feared that Charles would use the same army against them. They issued a militia ordinance that represented a clear challenge to royal sovereignty and stated the king's responsibility to the kingdom's defense. In January 1642, the king issued an order for the imprisonment of five leaders of the radicals from the House of Commons. The five managed to escape, but a civil war broke out as a response to the king's attempt against Parliament.

The king was defeated. However, a second civil war broke out in 1648 between Parliament's Puritans and the radical Protestant soldiers. The Protestants were victorious, and they sent Charles I to trial in January 1649, when he was condemned and executed as a tyrant, traitor, and public enemy of the commonwealth. Before this event, the accusation of treason had been reserved for those who committed crimes against the Crown. But now, under a new military order with Oliver Cromwell at its head, treason was defined as the Crown's betrayal of the people.

The radical Protestants started their experiment with a republican regime in 1649, and it lasted until 1660, a period known as an interregnum. Soon, Cromwell faced the same problems as the king. He needed to gather money for the emergencies caused by civil war, but Parliament proved to be nothing more than a frustration. Oliver Cromwell started collecting taxes without the consent of Parliament, and he started arresting his opponents without showing due cause. When people appealed to the Magna Carta for protection, Cromwell ridiculed the document, often mocking it in crude language.

Two years after the death of Oliver Cromwell, in 1660, Charles II claimed the English throne. Even though royal rule was back, Charles couldn't simply refuse to accept all the constitutional changes that the Long Parliament had made during the civil war. He accepted the limitations placed on the king's power, but still, there was no clear definition of which domain of government belongs to the king and which to Parliament. The settlement that restored the king in England was a victory for the Magna Carta's principle of law limiting the king's power, although the victory was limited. The common law could only check the royal prerogative, not completely ban it.

The first parliament session after the crowning of Charles II in 1660 enacted legislation that ratified some of the principles of the Great Charter. General taxes now always needed parliament's approval but were also extended to other royal attempts to raise money, such as customs duties. Knights' fees and military tenures were abolished, leaving the king without his feudal sources of income. However, some royalists rose to complain about these yolks on the king's executive power, and the Commons answered by acting against the individuals who did not respect the Magna Carta. Judges, who stayed in the king's employment, often mocked the Magna Carta, stating that they were above it did not have to live by it. Such individuals were accused of endangering the people's liberties and had to make a public apology to Parliament.

The question of sovereignty remained unanswered during the rule of Charles II, mainly because he made certain it was never asked. He was unwilling to risk falling to the same fate as his father and, therefore, avoided provoking Parliament. Parliament stayed quiet, too, unwilling to press the king to solve the matter. In this way, both parties continued to work in a balance of powers, avoiding stirring the political scene of England, which had just ended its experimental phase as a republic.

It was during the rule of James II that the demand for resolving the sovereignty question arose. The brother and successor of Charles II, he incited a crisis in 1686 by reviving the Court of High Commission, a supreme ecclesiastic court in England established during the rule of Elizabeth I that had proclaimed Puritanism an offense. This court was dissolved in 1641 by the Long Parliament, and now, in James' vision, he had revived it. The Court of High Commission was no longer prosecuting Papists and Puritans; instead, it served as a means for Catholicism to infiltrate into the Anglican church. James manipulated various laws to appoint his Catholic co-religionists into government positions that were reserved only for those who belonged to the Anglican church. Royal propaganda used the Magna Carta, calling on the freedom of religion guaranteed by the Great Charter. The king's opponents were forced to fight against the freedom of religion as, by admitting it, they would confirm that it was in the king's domain to make and unmake laws.

When the royal son of James II was born, his opponents were angered that Catholic rule would continue, as they hoped the crown would pass to one of the king's daughters who were married to Protestant princes. To make sure no Catholic line would rule England, they invited James' eldest daughter Mary and her husband, William of Orange, head of the Dutch Republic, to come and take the crown as joint rulers. William accepted the invitation, accusing James of breaking the law and disrespecting the Magna Carta. William came to England in 1688 with an army to challenge James, but the king suddenly lost all his support and was forced to flee to France. The act of abandoning England was considered equal to abdication, and Parliament declared the post of monarch vacant. William and Mary were crowned as joint rulers, and the parliament assembly chose to ignore the old English customs of hereditary law that called for only male successors. By doing so, they changed the constitution and showed that the power they wielded was greater than the monarchs.

A new Magna Carta that would better define the rights of a king and the rights of his subjects was debated. The Bill of Rights was drafted and enacted in December 1689. The bill was a pragmatic document, as was the Magna Carta. It responded to the specific problems of James II's rule, listing twelve unlawful acts that James had committed followed by fifteen measures for correcting his wrongs. The king's right to issue decrees with the force of law was denied by this bill, and he was prohibited from gathering or levying taxes without Parliament's approval. It made it illegal for a king to have a standing army without the consent of Parliament, and the people were guaranteed their rights of jury trials. The coronation oath was reworded by another act to make sure the king would obey not only traditional law and customs but also the statutes of the Parliament–once more showing that the king would always be overpowered by Parliament if the need should arise. The possibility of an absolute monarchy in England died as Parliament made itself superior to the king. The Magna Carta continued to inspire Parliament, which issued writs and statutes that would grant more and more liberties to the people of England.

# Chapter 11 –The New World and the Magna Carta

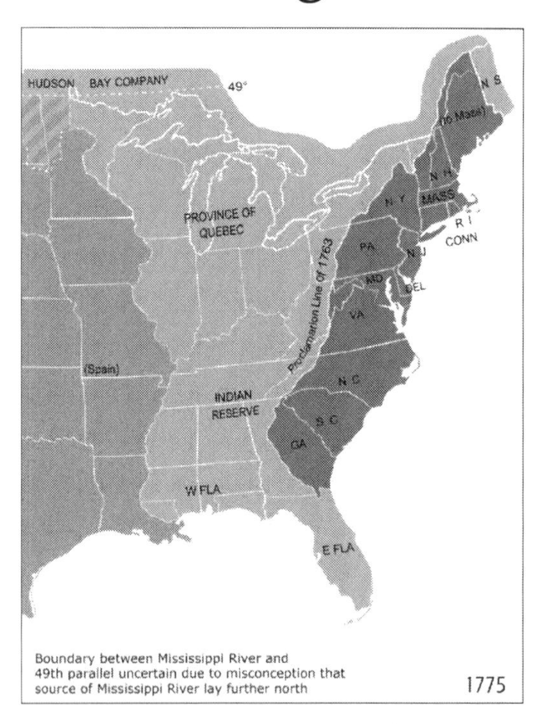


The Thirteen Colonies (red)

Source:https://en.wikipedia.org/wiki/Thirteen_Colonies#/media/File:Map_of_territorial_growth_1775.svg

English common law and its liberties started spreading all over the globe during the expansion of the British Empire. However, the

Magna Carta was not accepted everywhere equally. New territories brought new people to the British Empire, and those people had their own centuries-old laws and customs. The Magna Carta was purely a British heritage, and it continued to thrive only in colonies whose citizens were mostly British. The Great Charter continued to live in Canada, Australia, New Zealand, and the United States. However, nowhere did English common law influence the whole nation as much as in the first thirteen colonies in North America. There, the Magna Carta took on a new life and directly influenced the shaping of a new nation, The United States of America.

The settlers in North America were convinced they were still regarded as citizens of England. Bringing the Magna Carta with them, they thought it would give them protection from arbitrary government. They considered the Great Charter a contract between themselves and the king, and this contract spelled out all the obligations for both sides. In 1606, King James I even issued a charter that confirmed the rights and liberties of the Virginia Company. The charter stated that colonists would enjoy the same liberties and immunities as the people of England. Massachusetts got its own similar charter in 1629 that promised liberties to the colonists as if they were born within the Kingdom of England.

In 1765 and 1774, a reaffirmation of the charters was needed. The colonists were promised that they could keep all the freedoms their immigrant ancestors brought to America. The promise was made by both the Stamp Act Congress and the First Continental Congress. The liberties included not just freedom itself but also common law, by which they had the right of a trial by jury.

All the charters given to the colonies had a clause that was directly drawn from Clause 29/39 of the Magna Carta. The clause promises that no man's life would be taken, no man would be imprisoned, banished, or dismembered, and no man's lands would be taken or damaged unless the law was broken. Over the next century, all colonies would be given similar charters, with astonishingly similar clauses, and they all guaranteed the same rights directly taken from the Magna Carta.

Because of these charters given to the colonies in America, the English books of law were in high demand, especially the works of Edward Coke on the Magna Carta. Philadelphia published the 1225 version of the Magna Carta as part of William Penn's tract. William Penn was the founder of the Quaker colony, later known as Pennsylvania. In 1681, King Charles II granted Penn a charter with which he brought freedom of religion to his Quaker colony. In the colonies of North America, the law became the most popular profession since it promised not only profit but also status in society. Many of the Founding Fathers of the United States were lawyers. Out of the fifty-six signed names on the Declaration of Independence, twenty-five belonged to lawyers. Among them, Thomas Jefferson is known for having the finest private library, with many English legal texts that offered their interpretations of the Magna Carta.

In the beginning, the colonies enjoyed privacy and were mostly left alone as the king and the English Parliament had little interest in them. For one hundred years, America was seen as nothing more than unprofitable new lands less valued than the sugar islands in the West Indies. But when the British Empire realized the American colonies' potential and tried to influence their economy, the people were already accustomed to their liberties. Suddenly, possession of America was regarded as the king's prerogative, and it was the king who decided to disallow the acts adopted by the colonial legislatures. Because the colonial legislatures had no clear relationship with the English Parliament, King George III dismissed their existence. It was the English Parliament that took upon itself the regulation of external trade. The members of Parliament started claiming that because possessions in America were gained either by conquest or by diplomatic measures with the native people, they did not fall under the jurisdiction of English common law. America was not a part of the motherland; therefore, America had no guarantee of enjoying the same rights and liberties. Soon, the English Parliament took authority over the colonies, claiming that they existed only to bring profit to the British Empire, and as such, must be taxed under separate economic policies. After the war with France (1755-1763), Parliament expected the American colonies to organize their own defenses and pay higher taxes, which now spread from trade to all aspects of life. The angered colonies were left with little choice but to fight to regain their freedoms. The Magna Carta was once more at the epicenter of the events, as the colonies often cited it in pamphlets and propaganda against the British Empire's government.

The first protests and uprisings started in 1765 when the English Parliament issued the Stamp Act, imposing more taxes on the colonists, especially for printed material. Newspapers, legal books, magazines, playing cards, and many other materials had to be printed on stamped paper produced in London. The stamp was a revenue stamp that had to be paid in British currency, not the colonists' paper money. The colonists implemented the slogan "no taxation without representation" in their fight to regain the liberty of no taxation without consent, which was guaranteed by the Magna Carta. Even John Adams, in his draft for the community protest, wrote that the stamp violated the British constitutional principle that no man would be taxed without his consent given in person or by a proxy. For him, the British government's actions directly conflicted with the Magna Carta. However, England did not react, and new taxes followed in 1767 and 1773 when the East India Company gained a monopoly on selling tea to the colonies. The colonists were outraged by these moves and decided not just to boycott the company's tea but to throw their ships' cargo into the sea in an event known as the Boston Tea Party. The protests that followed were violent, and Parliament was pushed into issuing the Intolerable Acts of 1744, by which they closed the Boston port and suspended the charter given to the Massachusetts colony in 1629. The goal was to punish Boston and set an example to other colonies of what would happen to them if they did not obey the English Parliament's authority.

The American armed rebellion that followed took as its precedent the uprising of the barons who had extorted the Magna Carta from King John. By the colonists' interpretation, the barons were heroes of popular liberty. The seal of Massachusetts was redesigned during these times to represent a militiaman with a sword in one hand and the Magna Carta in the other. In fact, the protesters combined their modern views of law and the traditional appeals of the Great Charter in their war against the Stamp Act. It was the natural law that pushed forward the political thought of the American revolutionaries. The Magna Carta was even cited in the Declaration of Independence, which was signed on July 4, 1776. The natural rights of life, liberty, and the pursuit of happiness found their place within the Declaration in the bold words of Thomas Jefferson. The Declaration continued with a statement that if the government threatens these natural rights, it is the people's right to alter or abolish said government. The Declaration continued by accusing the king of breaking the contract between himself and the colonists when he took away the charters granted to America. He was also accused of staging a war against his own people, who had left England as free men only to become slaves, losing their basic rights as citizens of the British Empire once they set foot in the colonies. King George III became the symbol of England's tyranny over its colonies, even though it was Parliament that came up with all the measures to profit from the Americas. This mistake wasn't unintentional. It was easier for people to grasp a fight against the monarchy, just as their forefathers had rebelled against it.

After the Declaration of Independence, the colonies finally considered themselves free of British rule and were ready to draft a new constitution that would replace the old charters. The common law of England was the basis on which they would continue building their own legal system, which would later be adopted by other colonies as they joined the United States of America. The need for English books of law once more grew, and America started printing material such as William Schley's *Digest of the English Statutes* from 1826. This particular work was commissioned by the Georgia legislature, and it included the entire 1225 Magna Carta text.

The American Revolution was a direct rejection of sovereign authority. With the ending of the war in 1783, the thirteen colonies were loosely bound together by the Articles of Confederation and Perpetual Union. However, it became clear that more centralized power was needed to keep the new states bound into a union. In 1787, the Constitution of the United States was born in Philadelphia, and out of it, a new centralized government came to be. The Founding Fathers made sure that this new government could not tyrannize the people of the United States of America but would be strong enough to protect them. The federal Constitution, which was adopted in 1789, was the compromise they came up with to guard the confederation as if it were a single state. The United States Constitution limited the government's power in more than one way. The Magna Carta gave a lesson on why the power of government needed to be constrained for the people to enjoy their liberties. To achieve this, the Constitution separated the government's power into three branches: the legislative, executive, and judicial. Each one of these branches was to act as a restraint to the others' power. The American Constitution also divided responsibilities between the federal government and the states. However, even though they restrict each other's power, it is exactly this division between federal and state sovereignty that has resulted in the conflict that lasts to this day.

As the federal Constitution came to light, the Anti-Federalists protested that there was no document to confirm the freedoms of the people, such as the Magna Carta. The supporters of the federation replied that there was no need for a new Magna Carta, as confirmation of the people's liberties was in the Constitution itself in the form of the first ten amendments known as the American Bill of Rights, ratified in 1791. The First Amendment went much further than the Magna Carta ever did in restraining the government. There was to be no official religion established, no abridgment of the freedom of speech or the press, and no prohibition of peaceable assembly or the petition for a redress of grievances. The Ninth Amendment promised that the enumeration of rights in the bill would neither restrain the people from gaining new rights nor bar them from defending their other rights. Americans had been oppressed by a monarchy and had developed a natural fear of history repeating itself. To prevent their government from acting similar to the English Parliament, they developed a series of constitutional documents that would guarantee their rights and protect them from ever being oppressed again.

It was the Fifth Amendment that was built upon the so well-known Clause 29/39 of the Magna Carta. It promised that no person would be deprived of life, liberty, or property without due process of law. The Sixth Amendment continued by borrowing exact phrases from the Great Charter, such as the "lawful judgment of peers" and "law of the land," while it promised a speedy trial by an impartial jury for those accused of crimes. Criminals gained the right to be informed of the nature of their accusations and the right to defend themselves.

Even though the Magna Carta influenced the Constitution and the Bill of Rights of the United States of America, it lost the central role in the court that it had held during the colonial times. It wasn't forgotten, though, as it was always the document that guaranteed due process to the people of America and, therefore, was held in high regard. Even a Supreme Court justice wrote about the significance of the Charter in 1819, speaking about the lessons mankind learned during the fight to defend their freedoms. The Magna Carta has been cited over a hundred times in Supreme

Court sessions, and even today's lawyers cannot resist citing it. For instance, during the famous 1994 sexual harassment case against American President Bill Clinton, the judge ruled against delaying the process during the president's term of office, calling on the guarantees that the Magna Carta gives to the people that even the sovereign is a subject to the law.

The United States Bill of Rights draws directly from the Magna Carta, promising freedoms to the people living on a continent that was unknown to King John or the barons. The Fifth and the Fourteenth Amendment are defined as "due process of law," which guarantees dignity, equality, and freedom to all people living in a republic, yet Americans proved that this concept is flexible.

For a long time, African Americans did not have the same rights and freedoms that were guaranteed by nature to the English settlers on the continent. It was only during the 1930s that the Supreme Court stepped outside the dogmas of earlier ages and revised the Bill of Rights to include citizens of other nationalities under its protections. During the late 1940s, people of African descent finally had the right to go to a public school, which had been reserved only for those of European descent. Segregation was approaching its end when, in 1946, the statues that divided passengers using public transportation were outlawed. However, the Supreme Court took its boldest step in 1954 when it finally admitted the full freedom and equality of African Americans by declaring racially-segregated schools unconstitutional.

The civil liberties in America were at the highest level of threat during the two world wars in the 20th century. During the wars, the restriction of freedom of speech was often tolerated, as was the roundup of radicals or people of "enemy" descent, who were often detained just for being of a certain nationality. For example, during World War II, people of Japanese descent were relocated and incarcerated in internment camps even though they were natural-born American citizens. Their liberties guaranteed by the Bill of

Rights were forcefully taken away. Internees often lost their property, as restrictions prohibited them from taking more than they could carry in their arms. Because of the relocation order, many people lost their jobs, and others were simply fired for being of Japanese descent. It was not until 1976 that American President Gerald R. Ford admitted that the internment of the Japanese was wrong and a national mistake. Civil Liberties Act of 1988 granted reparations to the Americans of Japanese descent who were affected by the actions of US government during the World War II.

# Conclusion

The remarkable story of the Magna Carta and its history will never come to an end simply because the document is still alive, well known, and widely celebrated. We, too, are part of its story, which will turn into history for the next generations. Even though the Great Charter changed many times throughout the ages and bears other names in many countries across the world, it still holds the same ideals of liberty that will keep pushing humanity forward.

In this book, the political process of the Magna Carta is fully on display. The reader can enjoy the story–with its remarkable characters–and through the story, the development of one of the world's greatest documents. Even today, humanity is asking the same questions regarding liberties as the barons of John's England, or the Edward Cokes of the Elizabethan and Jacobean eras. Considering the present age, the Magna Carta may seem to be an old institution that is crumbling under the pressure of greedy oligarchs and despots, but its principals, ideas, and guarantees are very much alive. Although we call it by a new name, the Constitution, the Great Charter continues to spread through all spheres of our individual lives. It still protects us from our own government in the same ways it protected the barons from the king's abuse of power. And it is a constant reminder of how everyone is equal in the eyes of the law, with no exemption–even for the rich and powerful.

As a founding cornerstone of the English constitution and the United States Bill of Rights, the Magna Carta is still observed as a bulwark that protects against arbitrary government. Interestingly, it is now celebrated with much more enthusiasm in America than in England. The American Supreme Court continuously cites the Charter, and it is not the only institution to do so. It is often cited in political debates, judicial discussions, and news media, be it in print or digital formats.

The Magna Carta showed its capacity to grow over time. From the barons' uprisings in the $13^{th}$ century to the American Revolution in the $18^{th}$ century, the Great Charter proved to be a resilient document. The original document underwent so many changes that what we have today can hardly be called the Magna Carta, but the original principals and ideas are still very much alive in today's statute books. By keeping the tradition of opposing the government's threats to the people's liberties alive, the Magna Carta has its role to play even today. It is still an inspiration to people who seek to overthrow the yolk of tyranny.

Here's another book by Captivating History that you might be interested in

# References

Davis, G. R. C. (1999). *Magna Carta.* London: British Library.

Holt, J. C., & Hudson, J. (2015). *Magna Carta.* Cambridge: Cambridge University Press.

Howard, A. E. D. (1968). *The road from Runnymede; Magna Carta and constitutionalism in America.* Charlottesville: University of Virginia Press.

Howard, A. E. D. (1998). *Magna Carta: text and commentary.* Charlottesville: University Press of Virginia.

King, E. (1988). *Medieval England, 1066-1485.* Oxford: Phaidon.

Linebaugh, P. (2008). *The Magna Carta manifesto: liberties and commons for all.* Berkeley: University of California Press.

Morris, M. (2015). *King John: treachery and tyranny in medieval England: the road to Magna Carta.* New York: Pegasus Books.

Bates, D. (2018). *William the Conqueror.* New Haven: Yale University Press.

Cohen, D. (1974). *The Black Death, 1347-1351.* New York: Watts.

Hadley, D. M. (2006). *The Vikings in England: settlement, society and culture.* Manchester, UK: Manchester University Press.

Leyser, H. (2019). *A short history of the Anglo-Saxons.* London: Bloomsbury Academic.

ROUTLEDGE. (2017). *Medieval England: an encyclopedia.*

Platt, C. (2013). *Medieval England: a social history and archaeology from the Conquest to 1600 Ad.* London: Routledge.

Saul, N. (2000). *The Oxford illustrated history of medieval England.* Oxford: Oxford University Press

Printed in Great Britain
by Amazon

61829788R00137